The Yorkshire 3 Peaks

A guide to the 3 Peaks Challenge

A history of the 3 Peaks area

Challenges beyond the 3 Peaks in the Dales

by

Jonathan Smith

"The best one day walking challenge in England"

Published by Where2walk

Copyright @ 2019 Jonathan Smith
The Right of Jonathan Smith to be identified as the Author of the work has been asserted by him in accordance with the Copyright, Designs and Patents Act 1988

All rights reserved. No part of this publication may be reproduced, stored in a retrieval system or transmitted in any form or by any means, electronic, mechanical, photocopying, recording or otherwise, without the prior permission of the author.

ISBN: 978-0-9956735-2-6

Every reasonable effort has been made by the author to trace copyright holders of material in this book. Any errors or omissions should be notified in writing to the author, who will endeavour to rectify the situation for any future reprints.

Designed and Published by Where2walk

Printed by Briggs Brothers, Keighley BD20 8LG

Pen-y-Ghent from Hull Pot

Contents

Map and Listing..6
Forward..8
Safety and Preparation in the Mountains...................12

The One Day Challenge, Route Details...............14
3 Peaks in 3 Days..36
History, Geology and Land Use..............................50
Not Just for Walkers...70
Beyond the 3 Peaks..84

Code of Conduct..106
Local Accommodation..108
About the Author...112

Map of the 3 Peaks Route

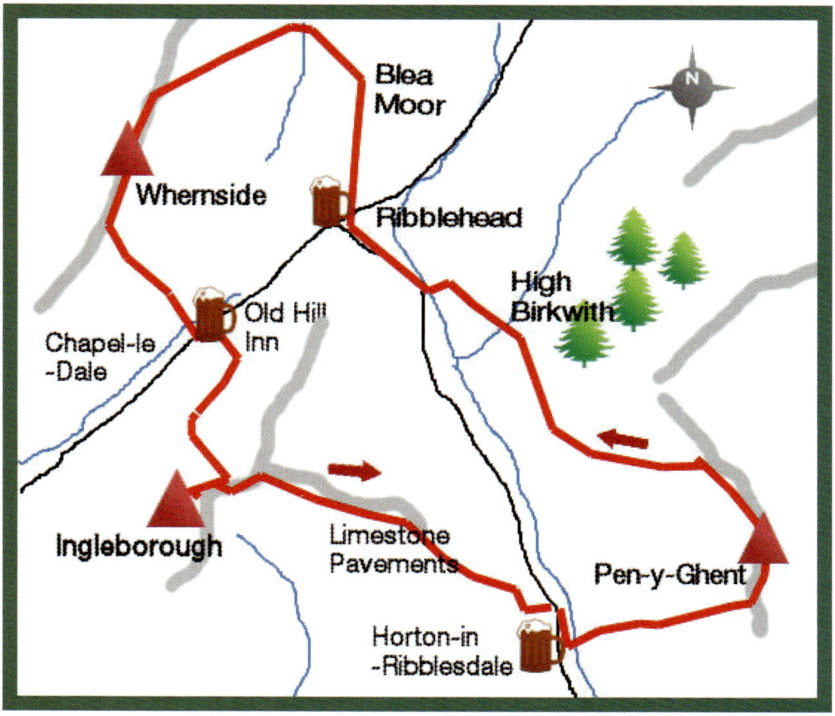

Philpin Farm with Whernside behind

Yorkshire 3 Peaks

1 Pen-y-Ghent

Pen-y-Ghent is isolated from the other two mountains and stands alone in most photos and descriptions. The shape is distinctive, the flat granite summit slope drawing the eye from miles around. To many it looks unclimbable, particularly on the approach from Horton. In fact it leaves a short scramble and a memory that is not forgotten.

The approach to Pen-y-Ghent

2 Whernside

Whernside is dominated by the conic Ribblehead viaduct on its southern, more popular, slopes but in reality has the least impressive profile of the 3 Peaks. However the image belies the true character of Whernside. Visit the northern slopes and your company will be the skylarks and lonely tarns with views north towards the Lakes and beyond.

Summit Ridge on Whernside

3 Ingleborough

The most popular of the 3 Peaks and rightly so. The mountain is full of interest whichever way it is approached. Limestone dominates the scene, spectacular pavements and scars, shake holes and caves pepper the hillside and are a delight to explore. The summit itself is flat topped, creating the same distinctive shape as Pen-y-Ghent, but covering a wider area.

Simon's Fell to Ingleborough

The Best 1 Day Challenge in England

Over 80,000 walkers take on the Yorkshire 3 Peaks Challenge each year; most complete it. Only the highest mountains in Britain have more climbers visiting their summits, Snowdon is the most popular but Scafell Pike, Helvellyn and Ben Nevis take over 100,000. However, as a challenge walk the Yorkshire 3 Peaks is the biggest of the lot, carrying over double the numbers of the National 3 Peaks (Ben Nevis, Snowdon and Scafell Pike).

The primary reason it is so popular is that it is achievable for the regular walker, even a less regular walker who is reasonably fit. The challenge is to complete the walk in a day. 12 hours is the 'official' target time but I have guided groups round that have taken over 16 hours and they have enjoyed it. Whether you take 9 or 16 hours the achievement is the same, it is each individual's milestone and the satisfaction of completing the walk is enormous.

Ribblehead at the weekend

In addition to being 'achievable' the area is relatively easy to get to, being on good public transport and Yorkshire itself easily accessible. A weekend involving travelling to Horton on a Friday night, doing the walk on Saturday and returning home on Sunday, is perfect for many working people. It is a great challenge for a charity walk (with many groups raising large amounts of money for worthy causes). It can also be a tick for a bucket list.

Finally, people are drawn to the beauty of the Dales or that is what you would expect. The reality is that, for most, the walk just happens to be in a lovely part of the country, it is the challenge that is the main focus.

The walk is not technically difficult, hands only having to be used twice, on a short step on Pen-y-Ghent and a similar one on Ingleborough. It is the sheer scale of the walk that makes it so difficult. Twenty four and a half miles is a long way, nearly a marathon, but harder, as it involves over 5,000 feet of climbing. Some of the paths are rough, despite the improvements that have been made over the last 10 years. The section downhill from Ingleborough to Horton is often rated the hardest of all due to the awkward and slippy exposed limestone rock.

It is this sheer length and the related fact that you are walking continually for 12 hours which makes it so unusual. Imagine a normal day, getting up to go to work at 7am, all the day entails, coming home having tea and settling in front of the TV at 7pm. On the 3 Peaks you will be walking all that time which is a sobering thought. It is not for the untrained and unfit. Turning up because that's what your friends and colleagues have suggested (and it sounds a laugh) is just not going to work.

Physical fitness is part of it but so is mental fitness. You are going to be exhausted, maybe above and beyond any exhaustion you have felt before, and you have to be able to cope. Many turn up having no idea what to expect and completely unprepared. Comfortable (not necessarily new) shoes, plenty of snacks, water and waterproofs are the essentials, add these to a positive mental attitude and a determination to keep going and most will make it.

Most people start at Horton in Ribblesdale and climb Pen-y-Ghent first, then Whernside and finish on Ingleborough. Between each mountain the route drops to a road so there are bail out points, one at Ribblehead (where there is a pub and train station) and one at the Old Hill Inn (where there is just a pub and a one and a half mile road walk to Ribblehead station). There is very little parking at the Old Hill Inn so starting with Ingleborough is not an option.

The National Park are responsible for the upkeep of the route and, over the years, have done an excellent job in making it both easier for the walker and preserving the environment from the terrible scars which were destroying parts of the route. It is better now but needs constant maintenance. Horton itself can become very busy on any given Saturday in the summer months, not a pleasant experience for walkers and locals alike. I often start my groups at Ribblehead where there is plenty of parking. I therefore tackle Whernside first.

Attracted by the Scenery?

Walkers should also be driven to the challenge by the beauty, heritage and splendid views. For most walkers this tends to be a secondary reason for taking the challenge. This book, as well as being a step by step guide to the route, hopefully adds some flesh and interest to the day. Raise your eyes at times from the path ahead, look around and appreciate the wonderful and unique scenery.

The Geology is fascinating, from exposed pavements to limestone scars under which is the best caving system in Britain. There is also the remains of the area's rich industrial history; the Settle to Carlisle railway and the extraordinary Ribblehead Viaduct are prominent, but you will also find signs of an Iron Age fort at the top of Ingleborough.

Take Time on the Mountains

One really special way to explore the 3 Peaks is to climb them all separately, come up for a holiday and complete the '3 Peaks in 3 Days' challenge. Take time to explore each mountain, climb them by a separate and maybe preferable route. It is a relaxing way of appreciating these three excellent mountains.

The Dales is not just about the 3 Peaks Challenge. There are other challenges in the area for those walkers wanting to return and enjoy the heritage and scenery of the area. In a neighbouring valley is the Wharfedale 3 Peaks, a similar challenge but over rougher paths, the main difference being you will hardly see a soul.

Whernside from Simon Fell

The 'Dales 30' are the 30 mountains over 2,000 feet within the Yorkshire and Cumbrian Dales. They include some of the best mountains in England such as the Calf, Buckden Pike and Great Knoutberry Fell. It is a great challenge either for a succession of one day walks and long weekends or as a continual ten day challenge, a tough way to spend a walking holiday but extremely satisfying. There is much to explore "Beyond the 3 Peaks".

The Final Word

I was guiding a small group over the 3 Peaks and as we approached Blea Moor Tunnel I noticed a number of photographers on the side of the path. Assuming a steam train was coming through on the picturesque Settle to Carlisle railway I asked when. In five minutes I was told. Perfect. We waited on the bridge just shy of Blea Moor tunnel and soon heard the familiar chug chug of a steam train and the plume of steam in the distance. The steam train passed directly under us, covering us with clouds of steam before disappearing in to the tunnel. The group (and myself) were mesmerised.

I received a note after the walk from the group leader thanking me for the day and it ended "it was only when the steam train came through that I started to look around, I was too focused on the walk before. It really is a completely unique landscape, great to look at definitely but also full of interest. You telling us a bit on the history of the area helped and took my mind away from the walk…at least for a while. I'll be back".

I couldn't put it better myself.

Yorkshire 3 Peaks

Summit of Pen-y-Ghent

Safety in the Mountains

The Yorkshire 3 Peaks involve climbing the highest mountains in Yorkshire. Even though the paths are obvious, the underfoot terrain can be poor and exhausting, rivers can provide dangerous crossings in spate and it is easy to become disorientated when the cloud comes down. Winter conditions are particularly dangerous; short days, frozen ground and snow slowing progress are typical difficulties.

This book is intended to be only a rough guide to the best routes up the mountains and not used as a 'one stop shop'.

Anyone climbing the Yorkshire 3 Peaks (or the other walks in this book) must be able to navigate using a map and compass (or have someone in the group who can). A

GPS can be used as an aid to a map and compass but not as a replacement. Mobile phones can also help but they are easily damaged, run out of battery and it is not always possible to get a signal.

Appropriate clothing should be worn and if walking on your own a second person informed of your route and likely return time. In groups always plan for the slowest member of the party.

Not only do these precautions help reduce (but not eliminate) any dangers, they will also make the walks much more enjoyable.

NOTE: The two most common reasons people do not complete the 3 Peaks are lack of fitness and blisters.

1. **Lack of Fitness:** This is a long day and is exhausting both physically and mentally. Coming unprepared without training will at best make the day very hard work and at worst failing to complete the challenge. In many cases one member of a group failing means the rest of the group fail too.

2. **Blisters**: Make sure you have done plenty of walking in your boots/shoes. An old comfortable pair is better than a new, untried pair. Regardless take some plasters or the ever reliable Compeed!

The Best Places to Stay

The most convenient places to stay are **Horton** (where most 3 Peakers start), **Ribblehead**, (where I sometimes start) and **Chapel le Dale**. In all of these places there are pubs, some bed and breakfast accommodation and camp sites/bunk barns.

However on weekends from May to September the accommodation fills up early in the year in these places and you may have to stay further afield. If you have a means of transport that can be the best option. **Settle, Skipton** and **Ingleton** have plenty of accommodation and a bigger choice of places to eat and drink after the walk.

Other villages I can recommend are **Long Preston, Clapham** and **Austwick.**

A list of accommodation is available at the back of this book.

Route Stops During the Day

During the day there are very few places to stop for refreshments or toilet breaks. There is nothing on the mountains themselves (this is not Snowdon with a cafe on the summit) so there are many hours between possible breaks.

Horton: Public toilets and two pubs. The 3 Peaks Cafe is presently closed (2019) but may well open for 2020 and beyond. Check before you arrive. The clocking in service was in the cafe so is also out of action.

Ribblehead: One pub (the Station Inn) and there may be a butty van, particularly at weekends but the days and times are not fixed.

Chapel le Dale: One pub (Old Hill Inn) and Philpin Farm which at present opens at weekends for refreshments and has a toilet.

Using the Settle to Carlisle Railway

For those taking on the challenge of the 3 Peaks either separately or in one go there are many ways of using the railway. The trains run approximately every two hours.

Arrive and depart by train and leave the car behind. Parking is a particular issue in Horton, arriving by train will help.

During the challenge day the stations at Ribblehead and Horton offer a 'get out'.

Step by Step Route Details

Yorkshire 3 Peaks

Final 3 Peaks summit but a long walk to Ribblehead

How to Use the Step by Step Guide

Dividing the Route into 6 sections

When I am guiding groups around the 3 Peaks Challenge I mentally subdivide the day into 6 sections. With the settlements on the road at Horton, Ribblehead and the Old Hill Inn providing obvious dividing points for a section I then add the summits as another. Each section therefore includes a climb or a descent of one of the 3 Peaks.

If each section takes two hours then that is a twelve hour round but of course each section is not the same length or difficulty, However it is a useful guideline.

Over the forthcoming pages each section has a spread which includes the following:

Summary

Step by step route description

Downloadable GPS coordinates

A sketch map

Photography

Interesting facts

Route Description

Each of the main 6 sections are split into a further 5 or 6 mini sections. The description describes these mini sections, mentioning anything useful or interesting as well as the key route changes.

The mini sections vary in length of walk and usually start and finish at a specific point where the route changes direction, meets a point of interest etc:

I have tried to add a few areas to look out for, good views, points of interest as otherwise a turn left/turn right route description becomes too bland.

Sketch Maps

Each of the 6 sections of the 3 Peaks route includes a sketch map. The sketch map is not 100% accurate in distances and information and should only be used as a basis for the walk. It must be used in conjunction with the route description and/or GPS route.

My own preference is to use the sketch map and convert the route on to either an Ordnance Survey Explorer (OL2) map or a Harvey map which are designed specifically for walkers.

GPS Route

I have downloaded the route details via a GPX mapping system and included the appropriate coordinates on each of the 6 sections.

I would suggest using this as the written route description ie: as a guide to the route but should be used in conjunction with a paper map (even as back up).

The number of coordinates reflect the key route decisions on the section.

Photos

I have included some photographs in each section which reflect unusual or noticeable sites on the route. There is so much of interest on the route it is easy to miss things.

Interesting Facts

I have described some interesting facts or things that walkers should be aware of in each section. For example it is worth spending a few extra minutes visiting the spectacular geological feature of Hull Pot on the descent from Pen-y-Ghent.

Step by Step: Pen-y-Ghent

Yorkshire 3 Peaks

The ascent of Pen-y-Ghent

Section 1. Climb Pen-y-Ghent

A steep but quick start with a good scramble near the summit

4.5km (2.7 miles)

Parking: there is a main car park with toilets which is the best start point. On some Saturdays this becomes full early but usually a local farmer opens out the field over the road bridge (for a cost). The 3 Peaks Café is the traditional start point and has a clocking in mechanism (closed in 2019).

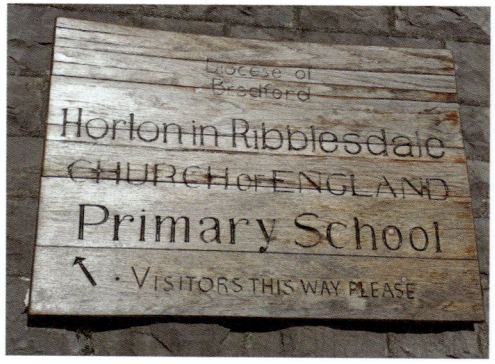

The primary school. Now closed.

1 Start at the car park. Head south on the main street in Horton past St Oswald's Church on the left and the Golden Lion pub on the right. Just past the pub the road turns sharply left. On your left a minor road heads towards Pen-y-Ghent with the river on your left.

2 Follow this tarmacked farm lane for ¾ mile. The lane soon passes the old Horton primary school on your right and enters some woodland. Just before reaching a farm house (fantastically named Bracken Bottom) a signpost points to the left through a small kissing gate on to the open hillside.

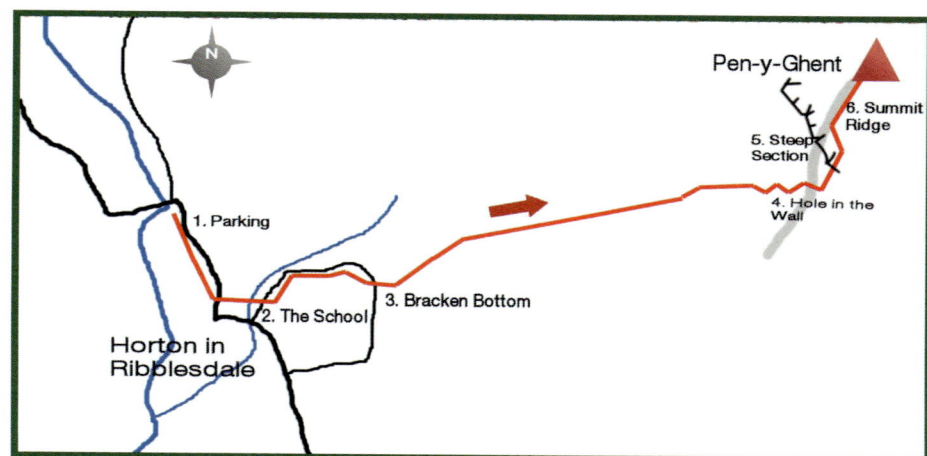

Yorkshire 3 Peaks

3 For just over 2km the footpath undulates towards Pen-y-Ghent, gradually climbing 270m. The path passes through three gates and a number of small limestone scars. There are many excuses to stop and look behind. Horton, the large limestone quarry at Moughton and the distinctive outline of Ingleborough, where you will be in many hours time, dominate.

4 After 2km the path comes to a small gate on the broad shoulder of Pen-y-Ghent. Here the 3 Peaks route meets the Pennine Way long distance trail. Turn left and you are confronted with the imposing edge of Pen-y-Ghent. Initially the climb is steep, the path soon bends away from the wall with steep land to your right. The mountain across the valley to your right is Fountain's Fell. There is some minor scrambling before the path returns towards the wall.

5 The path then climbs steeply towards the final section of the climb. There is one awkward step where you will need to use your hands before the path emerges on to the summit plateau. This final step is where the limestone makes way for the gritstone cap of the mountain.

6 From here there is a pleasant 300m walk to the summit trig point. The summit at 694m has a walled shelter and a small step stile to the west side of the wall. The views towards Fountain's Fell and north west into lovely Littondale are really pleasing.

Finger posts at 'the Hole in the Wall'

GPS Route

SD 8082 7261
SD 8112 7216
SD 8168 7225
SD 8300 7273
SD 8364 7277
SD 8371 7306
SD 8385 7337

Factory Made Footpaths

As you approach the summit of Pen-y-Ghent look at the large paving stones on the footpath. These are stones renovated from the local cotton and wool mills. Many of the slabs contain holes for fittings and chunks of metal where the mill slabs were locked together.

Section 2. Descend Pen-y-Ghent

A long, time consuming section with the trickiest navigation.

12km (7.5 miles)

1 On the far side of the wall from the trig point head north west for 100m to some wide stone steps. These steps are part of the repairs to the route (2018) where the hillside was badly scarred over a wide area. Descend the steps and follow the path as it turns north with some steep land to your left. Continue along the path for 500m to a sharp left turn. A faint path carries on, ignore this, it was the old 3 Peaks route.

Hull Pot in flood

2 From the sharp bend, follow the wide path as it drops gradually downhill for 1.5km, through a small kissing gate and a meeting of paths. Turn left to Horton, turn right to Hull Pot but the 3 Peaks route carries straight on.

3 A short, sharp climb on a recently repaired path leads to Whitber Hill. The area is wild but the path straightforward as it continues north west. After 2 small gates the path drops west to meet a major track. This is part of the Pennine Way.

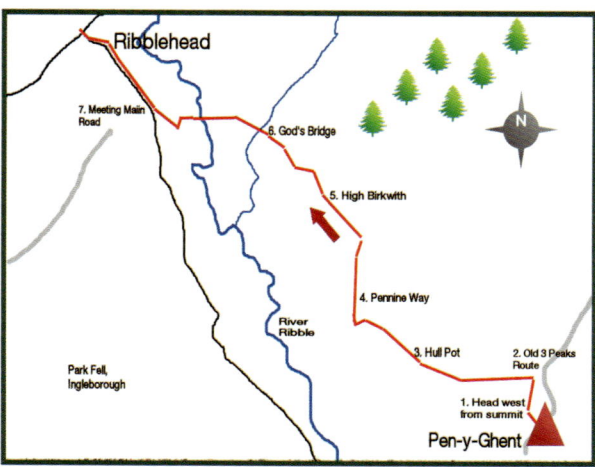

4 Follow the Pennine Way for 1km to a well signposted stile to your left. Leave the Pennine Way and take the left path, signposted 3 Peaks. Initially follow the wall for 300 metres but where the walls meet go through a step stile and continue north west with some impressive limestone pavements to your left.

Yorkshire 3 Peaks

5 After the limestone pavement (with the farm of High Birkwith to your left) the path carries on north past some trees to your left and alongside a wall for a few metres. Cross the obvious farm track and follow the eroded grassy bank directly ahead as it drops briefly and then climbs on a walker's path. It can be muddy here but only lasts for 200m till meeting another farm track with a wall to your left. This track leads to God's Bridge over Brow Gill Beck after 200m.

6 From God's Bridge continue along the widening track north west for 500m to the buildings at Nether Lodge. Keep to the right of the house, cross a small footbridge and arrive at the main farm track leading just north of west from Nether House. Follow this track for nearly 2km, over the River Ribble and through the haunted farm buildings of Ingman Lodge (try it at night!). The track emerges on the B6479, the road between Horton and Ribblehead.

7 Turn right and follow the intermittent grass verge to the T junction at Ribblehead, over 1.5km away. Here there is often a Butty van and always cars and people milling about (resting!).

The long crossing from Pen-y-Ghent

GPS Route
SD 8385 7337
SD 8383 7240
SD 8229 7429
SD 8102 7487
SD 8104 7612
SD 8038 7699
SD 8003 7727
SD 7940 7781
SD 7776 7809
SD 7657 7928

Hull Pot

100m to the north of the 3 Peaks route lies Hull Pot, a collapsed underground cavern. It is not as a cave that it is impressive but as a waterfall, particularly in wet conditions. The water finds its way underground to appear lower down the hillside but in very wet conditions the hole fills up and overflows creating a particularly dramatic sight.

Step by Step: Whernside

Yorkshire 3 Peaks

Crossing the aqueduct next to Blea Moor Tunnel

Section 3. Climb Whernside

The highest mountain approached via a circuitous route.

7km (4.4 miles)

1 From the road junction take the obvious path heading directly for Ribblehead Viaduct. Follow the path on its east side but take a few metres detour to stand under this impressive structure built by the Victorians (for more information on Ribblehead Viaduct turn to pages 62 and 63).

Blea Moor Junction near Ribblehead

2 Climb a short slope next to the north end of the viaduct and follow the path on the east side of the railway for 2km. To your left is Blea Moor station (disused) and two foot bridges/stepping stones over Little Dale Beck. The footpath crosses over the rail line just before it disappears in to Blea Moor Tunnel. This is the Settle Carlisle railway, one of the most beautiful lines in Britain, particularly inspiring if you are fortunate to catch a steam train entering the tunnel. Also look to your left to the pretty waterfall at Force Gill on the slopes of Whernside.

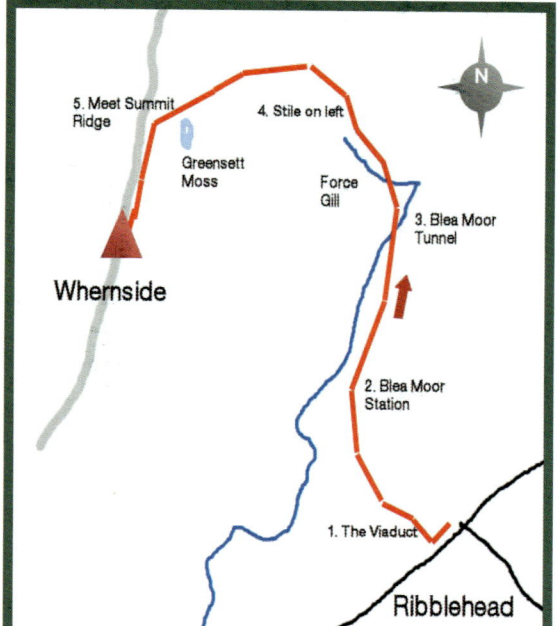

3 From here the climbing starts. Head just west of north for 900m until there is a stile to your left with a footpath signed and heading towards Whernside. The height climb to the stile is 110m.

26

Yorkshire 3 Peaks

4 The track you are on continues to Dentdale but you need to go over the stile and follow the path which gradually bends more westerly and climbs steadily. After 1km the path leaves a wall to your right and becomes large stone slabs. This used to be one of the boggiest sections of the route but thankfully no more. The path climbs steeply onto the long summit shoulder of Whernside.

5 The summit is just short of 1km further south along the ridge (bounded by a wall on your right). The views to the east (your left) are very impressive from the lonely Greensett Moss Tarn just below, over Ingleborough and back all the way to Pen-y-Ghent, thankfully now in the far distance. The summit has a trig point on the other side of the wall and a shelter on your side. At 736m (2,415 feet) it is the highest point in Yorkshire. There are good views to the north west over the Howgills and the southern Lakes.

Greensett Moss from the summit ridge

GPS Route
SD 7657 7928
SD 7602 7948
SD 7610 8167
SD 7572 8245
SD 7531 8269
SD 7481 8266
SD 7410 8236
SD 7385 8139

Tarns of Whernside

There are not many tarns in the Yorkshire Dales but Whernside has most of them! As well as Greensett Tarn which can clearly be seen on the ascent of Whernside to your left there are 3 good sized tarns on the western side of the summit ridge. Half way along the ridge is a stile which leads to the Access Land and some excellent views across the 3 tarns and into Dentdale. It is a lovely and quiet place to wander around when there is more time!

Section 4. Descend Whernside

A short section but with the trickiest and steepest descent.

4.5km (2.8 miles)

1 From the summit continue along the eastern side of the wall for 1.25km. The summit ridge is like the keel of an up turned boat and you are now obviously on the down side. Pass through a double gate and then the path becomes increasingly rough as steeper, short sections are mixed with longer flatter ones.

The Highest Place in Yorkshire, Whernside summit

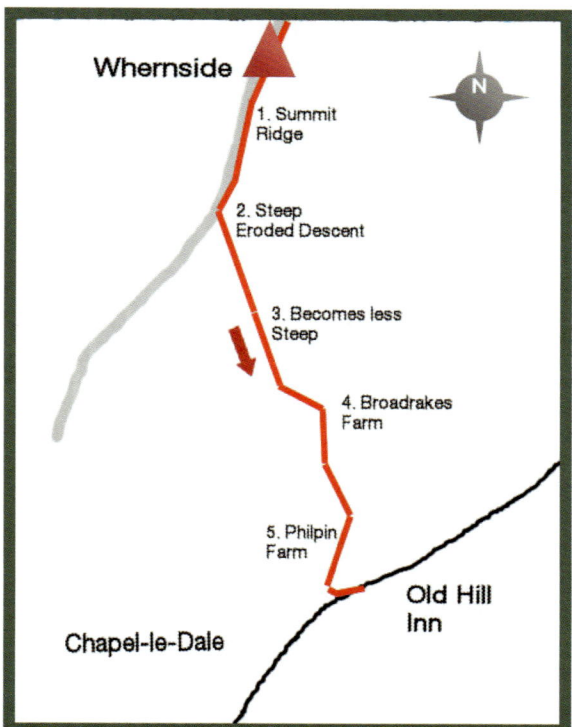

2 The main 3 Peaks path leaves the summit ridge to the left. The less distinctive path continues along the ridge for a further 3km before dropping down through the waterfalls to Ingleton. The 3 Peaks path now becomes steep and awkward as it drops down in what prior to 2018 was an increasingly badly eroded path. It is the worst section of the route. In early 2019 repairs have been made to the path with the use of large boulders providing a series of steps. It is an improvement and certainly safer, but aesthetically it needs more time to bed in (refer to pages 64-67 on the efforts to improve the footpaths across the full 3 Peaks route).

Yorkshire 3 Peaks

3 After the initial steep drop of 100m there is a small gate and the path, albeit still rough in places, improves and the land becomes less steep. Pass through a second gate and continue downhill to a third gate just after a pleasant section of limestone pavement on your left.

4 After passing through the gate take the first, almost immediate, left turn and pass some farm building on your left. Join the tarmacked road heading south from the buildings across open fields. After 750m of easy walking the road crosses a stream and bends to the right. A short climb brings you to Philpin Farm. For the past few years the farm has been very welcome, providing toilets and refreshments served from one of its barns. A great initiative and long may it continue.

5 150m beyond the farm the farm road meets the main Ingleton to Ribblehead road. Turn left and walk up to the Old Hill Inn. Be aware the present owners do not allow walkers into the toilets without purchasing in the pub, use the Philpin Farm toilets if necessary.

Philpin Farm near the Old Hill Inn

GPS Route
SD 7385 8139
SD 7347 8024
SD 7354 8001
SD 7392 7904
SD 7410 7839
SD 7427 7783
SD 7439 7768

Philpin Farm

The refreshment stop at Philpin Farm is an extremely popular and welcoming spot, situated almost mid way between Whernside and Ingleborough. The refreshments can be a real bonus. I often don't tell my groups so it comes as even more of a pleasant surprise. It is open weekends from May to the end of September (check though). It is also a great example of diversification from a farmer looking to increase their income.

Step by Step: Ingleborough

Yorkshire 3 Peaks

Sulber Nick near Horton with Ingleborough in the distance

Section 5. Climb Ingleborough

A delightful walk through the limestone followed by a sting in the tail.

4km (2.5 miles)

1 Just past the Old Hill Inn on your right hand side is a narrow step stile leading on to some open sloping land. Cross the slope and join a farm track with a wide gate to your right. Follow the farm track through the gate. Pass through a further 2 gates before entering the protected Southerscales Nature Reserve.

Southerscales Nature Reserve

2 Southerscales is an area of impressive limestone pavements and a large shake hole (crater) on your left, Braithwaite Wife Hole. After the path bends to the right it passes through another gate and the underfoot terrain immediately changes from a wide path to peat bogs.

3 The path for the next 1km would have been purgatory in the past (particularly in the wet) but now a series of stone slabs and duck boards make the crossing of the peat much easier. The route climbs steadily, crosses a stream, until it reaches the bottom of a very steep section, the 'sting in the tail'.

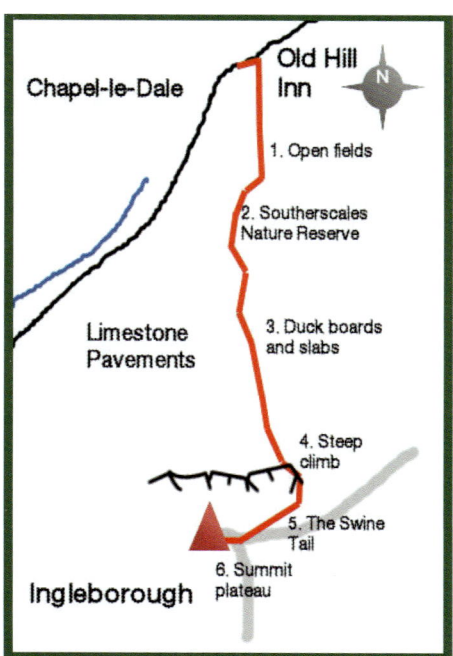

4 The 100m climb zig zags up a steep path next to a stream on your right, even necessitating the use of hands towards the top. It is not difficult but when walkers have come this far it can be a real struggle. At the top of the path, cross the stream and pass through a kissing gate and on to the final climb to the summit.

Yorkshire 3 Peaks

5 From the gate the path climbs steadily west on a mainly paved path until it reaches the 'Swine Tail' just short of the summit plateau. Here stone steps have been engineered into the mountain side, improving the access. The path approaches the summit plateau on its right hand side, emerging on the plateau at its north east corner.

6 The plateau itself is roughly triangular in size and 300m long. It is also completely flat and rocky with no real paths. It is the most likely place where a compass may be needed in bad weather. From the top of the path head WSW for 200m to the large shelter, two cairns and a trig point situated just to the south. If you have no compass follow the northern rim of the plateau and where it bends slightly to the right turn left to the shelter. In good weather the views to the west reach the sea at Morcambe Bay.

The 'Sting in the Tail'. The final steep section

GPS Route

SD 7439 7768
SD 7445 7745
SD 7434 7697
SD 7429 7610
SD 7469 7502
SD 7472 7481
SD 7436 7464
SD 7409 7460

The Summit of Ingleborough

The summit plateau of Ingleborough has many structures. The cross ways shelter is the largest (and 2 tiered) and the trig point are joined by two very large cairns. One of the cairns marks the remains of a hospice tower built in 1830, which legend has it partly collapsed during the drunken opening ceremony.

Section 6. Descend Ingleborough

The finish is still a long way but the scenery is impressive.

8km (5 miles)

1 Return the 200m from the shelter to where you arrived at the summit plateau, using the northern edge as a guide if necessary. There is a cairn to mark the point where the path leaves the plateau. After 15m the path divides. Leave the outbound path and fork right. The path is rocky at first (although recently improved) and drops steadily to a nearly dry small tarn where the land starts to level out.

Limestone pavement on the route from Ingleborough

2 The next 1km is on a good path and gradually descends. Simon Hill (a Dales 30 mountain) lies to the left with Gaping Gill to the right. Pass over a stile and continue for another 500m until a wall appears on the left and some exposed limestone to the right. There is a ruined stone shooting barn to the left and then a stream crossing and a wooden gate with a sign for Horton. Keep following the wall on your left to another gate.

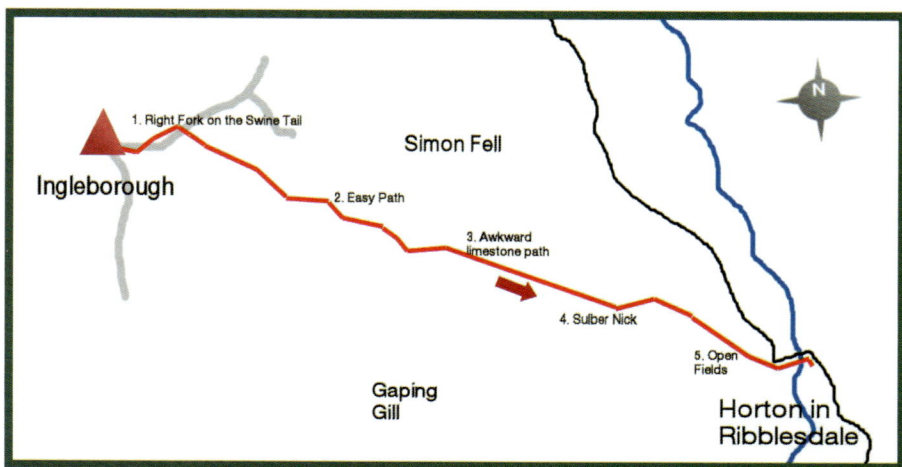

Yorkshire 3 Peaks

3 From here the path passes into a protected limestone area (Ingleborough Nature Reserve). Some of the walking through the reserve is on exposed limestone rock which after rain can be extremely slippy. After a long day it can be soul destroying. The path arrives at a crossing of paths at Sulber with a distinctive finger sign pointing to Horton in Ribblesdale.

4 The path follows the small gully of Sulber Nick in a ESE direction through another small gate to another sign for Horton. The path picks its way down the hill and through the limestone with the first houses of Horton in the distance. 1km from your final destination is a gate with a large information sign concerning the limestone that you have walked through.

5 From the gate the path undulates south east through another 2 gates. On emerging from the second gate take the short, steep final descent leading to Horton station. Cross the lines and enter the village at a sharp bend in the road. Head straight on to the bridge over the River Ribble (and the Crown Inn) and turn right into the car park.

Celebrating at The Crown

GPS Route
SD 7439 7768
SD 7436 7464
SD 7474 7466
SD 7587 7419
SD 7688 7367
SD 7779 7349
SD 7909 7316
SD 8038 7258
SD 8077 7261

Ingleborough Nature Reserve

The reserve is an Area of Special Scientific Interest as well as being an important conservation area, 1,104 hectares in size. Where the limestone is near the surface there is an impressive display of nature and wildlife. In particular wild flowers abound but also bog habitats such as hair's tail cotton grass, roe deer, beautiful butterflies and curlew birds. You may be too tired to appreciate all that is there (a good reason to return) but there are also small herds of rare breed cows, you will notice them!

One a Day: Pen-y-Ghent

The following pages discuss in more detail the individual mountains and the most enjoyable & leisurely walks up each of them.

Yorkshire 3 Peaks

Pen-y-Ghent from Hull Pot

One a Day: Pen-y-Ghent

Pen-y-Ghent

6 miles (490m/1,610ft climb)

There are 2 possible approaches to Pen-y-Ghent; the popular (and best) approach is from Horton in Ribblesdale (described below).
An alternative is to follow the Pennine Way from Dale Head Farm to the south.

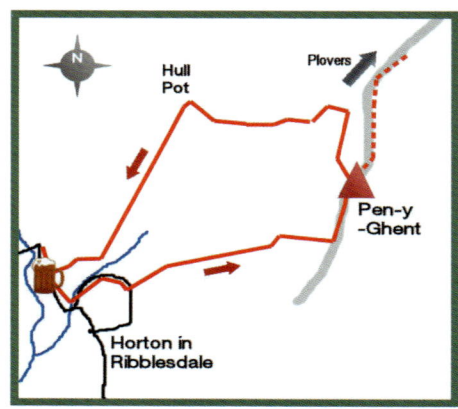

1 From the car park turn right and walk south along the road to the church. Just before the church a narrow path heads left past the church and then some houses to arrive at the river. A footbridge crosses the river, turn left on to a tarmacked road, pass the old school on the right and walk up the road for 750m to the farm at Bracken Bottom.

2 Just before the farm buildings turn left, pass through a gate and arrive on the open hillside. Keeping the wall to your left the obvious footpath undulates uphill for 2km. The path passes through 3 gates and outcrops of limestone before reaching an obvious 'Hole in the Wall'. This is the ridge of Pen-y-Ghent and where the path meets the Pennine Way.

3 From the Hole in the Wall turn left. Ahead is the daunting rocky climb up Pen-y-Ghent. Follow the obvious path which climbs through the rock. There is one point towards the crest of the ridge where hands are useful but in the main its bark is worse than the bite. Sooner than anticipated the crest is reached and the path flattens out, from here a simple 300m walk will bring you to the summit.

4 Pass over a stile to the west side of the wall. Initially the path is not easy to spot but head north west for 100m. As the land starts to drop the path becomes a series of steps (recent repairs from the National Park) put in to protect the surrounding land. From the steps the path becomes obvious and contours the hillside as it bends to the right. Follow the path (steep land to your left) to a sharp bend to your left. From here the path improves and offers an easy descent for 1.5km.

5 After a 2nd gate and before the path looks to climb there is a crossroads of paths. To the right is Hull Pot, straight ahead is the continuation of the 3 Peaks route to Ribblehead but through a gate to the left is the lane which leads to Horton. The wide track is rough in places but it is impossible to go wrong as it heads straight for 2km and then bends to the right before arriving at the main road in Horton.

Yorkshire 3 Peaks

The summit Trig Point

Having Time to Visit

1. Extending the walk to Plover Hill and Foxup Moor

I thoroughly enjoy extending the walk by including Plover Hill (a Dales 30 mountain) and dropping off the ridge north to join the path linking Littondale to Ribblesdale. The extra 5km is well worthwhile.

From the summit of Pen-y-Ghent head north along the wall (keeping it to your right). The route drops to a wide, shallow col which can be wet before turning north east and climbing steadily towards the small summit cairn of Plover Hill. The path bends back to the north before dropping 200m steeply off the summit plateau.

Turn left onto a bridlepath heading west. This path contours the hillside, gradually turning south towards Horton. The path meets the original route at the cross roads near Hull Pot.

2. Hull Pot

To the north of the cross roads where the 3 Peaks route leaves the descent to Horton lies Hull Pot, a near 100m long collapsed cavern in the limestone bedrock. It is highly impressive in all conditions but particularly so after heavy rains when the pot starts to fill.

In dry weather the water appears from the middle of the rock, an interesting example of how water has affected the limestone scenery of the area and created a unique landscape.

3. Horton Quarry at Moughton

On the west side of Horton a short walk takes you to the impressive limestone quarry under the cliffs of Moughton. It may have destroyed the hillside above Horton and many see it as an eye sore on the climb up Pen-y-Ghent but there is something impressive about the vast scale of the quarry.

One a Day: Ingleborough

Yorkshire 3 Peaks

The large summit area on Ingleborough

One a Day: Ingleborough

Ingleborough (from Clapham)

8 miles (615m/2,017ft climb)

The best approach to Ingleborough is from Clapham. Start at Clapham car park (SD 745693) with toilets.

Two further Ingleborough climbs are on pages 44 & 45

1 Turn right out of the car park and walk for 100m before crossing the river and turning right again to the entrance of the Ingleborough Estate. Here there is a choice, for a small fee walk the lovely wooded footpath past Clapdale Lake to Ingleborough Cave (see opposite) or head up the road for 30m to a wide track which in essence skirts the woods and avoids the fee. I would pay the fee and head through the estate.

2 The estate path is well signposted, initially next to the lake and then through the woods for 1.5km before bursting out of the woods near Ingleborough Cave. The path continues for a further 500m before turning sharply left into Trow Gill. Exit this steep sided limestone gorge through a narrow gap before continuing along a good footpath before reaching a double stile in the wall on your left. Cross it.

3 From the stile a good track leads towards Little Ingleborough (Ingleborough itself is seen to the right). Little Ingleborough is only 1km distant but a steep climb of over 230m. A detour to your right will bring you to the famous caving network of Gaping Gill (see opposite). From the little cairn at Little Ingleborough turn due north and walk the broad ridge towards the summit plateau.

4 After a few scrambling steps through a rocky scar the path emerges on the east end of the flat summit area of Ingleborough. It is 220m just north of west to the shelter, trig point and large cairn. Reverse your route from the summit off the plateau and along the ridge to Little Ingleborough.

5 A few metres past the cairn a faint track to your right heads just west of south down grassy slopes. This is a long descent with little of note aside from the wonderful views across the Forest of Bowland. This is Newby Moss. After 4km the path joins a farm track and arrives at the old road between Ingleton and Clapham at Newby Cote farm. Turn left and continue for 2km into the centre of Clapham.

Yorkshire 3 Peaks

From Little Ingleborough

Having Time to Visit

1.   Gaping Gill

It is barely a 10 minute detour to take you to the wire fence that surrounds Gaping Gill (take care most of the area is unfenced!). Gaping Gill is an underground cave which could comfortably fit the nave at York Minster inside. It is 130m long and 30m wide and Fell Beck which falls 100m into the cave is twice the drop of the Niagara Falls. The water from the beck disappears in to a vast network of caves and caverns before reappearing at Ingleborough Cave.

It is possible at certain (limited) times of the year to descend into the cave courtesy of the Caving Clubs. In 2018 I was lowered by the Craven Club. It was wet, cold but magnificent.

2.   Ingleborough Cave

Ingleborough Cave is probably the best show cave in the area, a well lit network of caverns and passages which has been available to the public for 180 years. The fossil gallery runs for much of the 500m of walkway and reflects the changing state of our climate through the ages including marine life and glaciation times.

The cave is open all year and tours are organised on the hour for a fee. I took my young children to Santa's Grotto where they were led by elves and received a gift from Santa himself!

3.   Clapdale

Just out of the village of Clapham the walk passes through the beautiful wooded valley of Clapdale. Whilst walking through the woods look out for some of the species of plants introduced by Reginald Farrer in the early 20th century. Reginald was part of the family Farrer who have owned the estate for the past 250 years and was a great botanist and traveller introducing such plant species as bamboo and Himalayan rhododendrons after a visit to the Far East.

One a Day: Ingleborough

Ingleborough
'The Traditional Way'

7.5 miles (680m/2,230ft climb)

From Ingleton a bridlepath heads directly east to the summit, the descent can be varied by heading north into the limestone above Raven Scar.

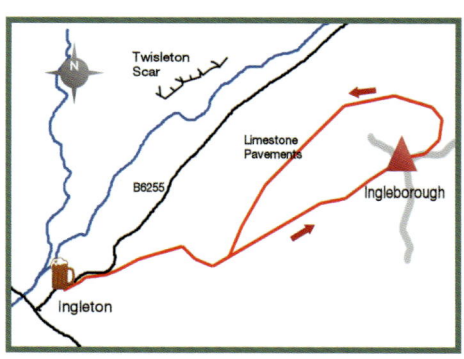

1 Climb out of the village on the B6255 to Hawes. Just past the old road to Clapham a bridlepath on the right hand side heads onto the hillside. This walled lane initially climbs steadily towards Ingleborough before leaving the walls behind and arriving at the farmhouse of Crina Botton, complete with a single wind turbine.

2 From the farm the path climbs more steeply, but continues on the line just north of east. On approaching the summit the path becomes rocky and eroded as it zig zags onto the final, large plateau of Ingleborough. The cairn, shelter and trig point lie at this end of the plateau.

Limestone above Raven Scar

3 It is possible to return directly back to Ingleton via the same route but I prefer to vary the descent and explore the limestone pavements above Raven Scar. To get here walk to the north rim of the plateau and follow it to a cairn that leads off the summit area. A steep descent heads down the 3 Peaks route and arrives at a stile. Pass through the stile and drop steeply along an eroded path, alongside a stream till it flattens.

4 From here leave the main path and head steeply downhill in a westerly direction. Gradually turn more south west and pick your own way into and through the limestone pavements (cliffs to your left). This is a delightful mile of walking until reaching the outbound track via a faint sheep track. This is all access land so you are free to walk off path.

Yorkshire 3 Peaks

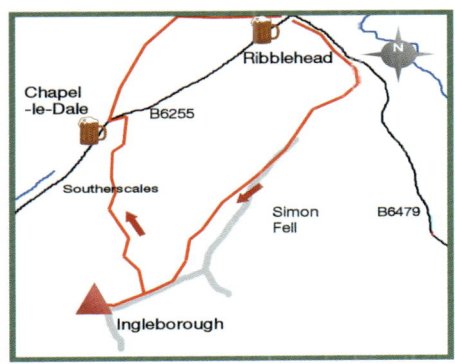

Ingleborough
'Via the Ridges'

9.5 miles (580m/1,900ft climb)

An interesting climb of Ingleborough involves a high level approach from Ribblehead over wide grassy ridges and a low level return.

1. From Ribblehead walk down the main road towards Settle for just over 1km. Leave the road at a track past some cottages and head directly up the steep hillside ahead. It is a daunting climb of 250m and over 1km to the trig point at Park Fell, a great place to enjoy the views towards Pen-y-Ghent.

2. From here the path follows a wall along the northern rim of the Ingleborough massif. After 1.5km a short excursion south will take you onto the Dales 30 mountain of Simon Fell. Bag the summit and return to the wall. After the path meets the main 3 Peaks Challenge route from the Old Hill Inn the path becomes paved as it picks its way to the summit plateau of Ingleborough. The highest point is 220m to the west marked by a large shelter, trig point and cairn.

3. Return to the point where you entered the plateau and follow the outbound route to a gate where the challenge route meets your outbound route. Follow the challenge route north down an initially steep, rocky path until it flattens and the path continues north. This path is the main 3 Peaks route as it passes through a gate into the Southerscales Nature Reserve. Where the path meets the road there is a choice.

Ingleborough from Simon Fell

4. Either follow the busy road back to Ribblehead (2.5km) or cross to the west of the Old Hill Inn and take the farm track towards Whernside (3km). Keep heading towards the viaduct via a bridleway, a second farm track to Gunnerfleet Farm and a final track to the viaduct. This route is slightly longer but more enjoyable and safer.

One a Day: Whernside

Yorkshire 3 Peaks

The Ribblehead Viaduct and Whernside

One a Day: Whernside

Whernside

8.5 miles (650m/2,130ft climb)

There are 2 possible approaches to Whernside; the popular route from Ribblehead (13km/8 miles) used and described on the 3 Peaks Challenge and the lesser known (more interesting) approach from Dentdale (13km/8 miles). It is the second walk described below.

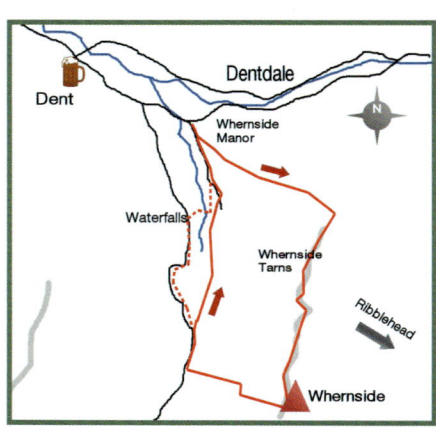

1 Park at Whernside Manor on the road up Deepdale. `A few metres further up the road from the parking area join a rough track leading up the slopes of Whernside to your left. Initially the track is used for access to the satelite aerials. The route continues to climb steadily for 2km before reaching the 'sheep pen' Boot of the Wold at 493m.

2 The main track carries on to Ribblehead but at the fourth (and last) wall on your right a faint path climbs steeply south alongside a wall. The path soon leaves the wall but continues north up to the 3 (or 4) Whernside Tarns. Feel free to leave the path as this is access land and head for a prominant cairn overlooking Dentdale. A great spot.

3 The path carries on south but is faint on the ground. Keep the tarns to your right. The track continues till it arrives at a stile at a fence on the summit ridge. You can either hop over to join the busy track on the east side of the wall or keep to the west side, largely trackless but lovely and peaceful.

4 The summit ridge is like an upturned boat running north to south. On arrival at the summit there are lovely views to the east with Ribblehead Viaduct, Ingleborough and Pen-y-Ghent prominant. From the summit take the faint path heading west, which heads steadily downhill. After the first steep section make sure you take the right hand path which leads to the corner of a wall. Follow the wall downhill to the road. There are some steep sections and a boggy area near its foot but stick close to the wall.

5 Follow the road downhill for 750m to a bend in the road, take the footpath leading straight on (north). This path now drops towards the foot of Deepdale and arrives at the farm of Deepdale Head. Keeping to the flank of Whernside continue through a number of fields (footbridges and stiles). Where the path splits keep to the low level path which soon arrives at Deepdale Beck. Just beyond, the path joins Dyke Hall Lane, follow the lane north for 750m back to the car.

Yorkshire 3 Peaks

The Whernside tarns

Having Time to Visit

1. Dent

I have often described Dent as a 'hidden gem', which would outgrow Malham in popularity if it was more accessible. Fortunately it is not and much the better for it.

The cobbled narrow streets of this small village (the only village in Dentdale) immediately strike any visitor to Dent but many of its best features are more hidden. In particular the church is worth exploring whilst the fountain of pink granite in the centre of the village commemorates Adam Sedgwick, born and educated in the village and one of the greatest geologists of all time. Black marble was actually mined in the valley and became famous throughout the land for its quality in fireplaces and other decorative features.

2. Waterfalls at Gastack Beck

Rather than leave the road at Point 5 continue down the road for a further 1km to a sharp bend in the road and the upper (and largest) waterfall of Gastack Beck. Then follow the stream down to return to the road and then leave by a footpath 200m further down where there is a series of pretty waterfalls and caves where the beck meets the larger Deepdale Beck.

A footbridge then takes you over Deepdale Beck and on to the main footpath. There are 6 falls of various size, one in a steep and narrow gorge, a second in a pretty dell, another feeding around a small boulder but all with a distinctive character.

History, Geology and Land Usage

Yorkshire 3 Peaks

Hull Pot on Pen-y-Ghent

History, Geology and Land Usage

The Yorkshire Dales has a presence (what I describe as a serene beauty) that makes it unique within Britain. However it is the landscape around the 3 Peaks that makes it distinctive and recognised throughout the world. This is largely due to the exposed 'white' limestone of the area, creating the pavements, escarpments and disappearing streams for which it is famous.

There is much more to the landscape than the limestone bedrock, the distinctive flat tops of the 3 Peaks are not matched by anything in the nearby Lake District, the wide glaciated valleys are a glaciologists dream (or an A Level geography student) and the deep river valleys an example of the power of water.

Today the most obvious influence on the views is the work of man and, in particular, the introduction of sheep to the landscape. Man's work however has been the direct result of the landscape they came to live in, one cannot function without the other.

Limestone scenery with Whernside behind

Bedrock of the 3 Peaks Area

1 The predominant rock type and the best known is the various layers of limestone laid out roughly 300 million years ago at a time when Yorkshire sat in a shallow sea near the equator. Limestone is formed by the calcium deposits from the shells of sea creatures which is then crushed over time.

2 The main limestone is recognized as carboniferous limestone and is roughly 200m in depth and provides the exposed white/grey rock so familiar to visitors to the area. More recently extra layers of limestone were added on top of the carboniferous limestone, providing a slightly different, greyer colour. This sandwich effect can be best seen on the flanks of the 3 Peaks, higher than the limestone formed in the carboniferous period.

3 Above the limestone and most noticeable on the summit plateaus of Pen-y-Ghent and Ingleborough is a layer of gritstone. This was formed by the sedimentary deposits of sands and gravels. It is known as Millstone Grit as a result of its use in corn mills and can also be seen all over the flanks of Ingleborough as large boulders, sitting incongruously on the lighter limestone bedrock. They look out of place.

4 It is the dominance of the exposed limestone as opposed to an outer level of Millstone Grit that characterises the 3 Peaks area, the rock being exposed by glaciation and weathering over the ages. Millstone grit is in its natural state further east near Upper Wharfedale and across to Nidderdale, the area around Great Whernside an excellent example…purgatory however for the walker.

5 A word too about the Craven Fault (or faults), a significant geological feature of the land near Ingleton in particular. Here the land has slipped and exposed the different levels of rock formation and helped create such recognisable features as waterfalls, cliff edges and most significantly exposing a layer of coal (roughly 6 miles by 4) near and under Ingleton. This coal was intensively mined in the mid 19th century, at one stage producing 16,000 tonnes per year.

History, Geology and Land Usage

Impact of the Glaciers

There have been a number of periods of glaciation over history but it is the most recent that has created the landscape that we see and know today. The Devensian Period of glaciation has lasted from 130,000 to 'only' 15,000 years ago.

The entire Yorkshire Dales was covered with ice during this period and the existing river valleys provided the outlet for the glaciers to scour their way up and down them. It is only the mountain tops including all 3 Peaks which stood atop the glaciers. On a day with a cloud inversion in the valleys it is quite possible to imagine the valleys as they were with great glaciers flowing below.

The recency (in geological terms) of the latest period of glaciation has meant that many features of the landscape are new and a perfect replication of a glaciated land. The U shaped valleys are perfect, all the main dales are beautifully formed and a geographer's dream. However, around the 3 Peaks the ice exposed the limestone bedrock, most noticeably with the limestone pavements of Ingleborough and to a lesser extent Pen-y-Ghent and Twisleton Scar on Whernside.

Limestone scar left by the retreating glacier

The limestone was also exposed on the mountain slopes when the ice retreated leaving the scars that are so characteristic of Ribblesdale and around Chapel le Dale. Another result of the retreating ice is the formation of drumlins, a mix of clay and shale left behind by the glacier and best seen around Ribblehead where they are aligned northwest/south east marking its directional flow.

Erratics are one of the oddest features of retreating glaciers. Here rocks are moved and dumped in different locations. On the pavements of Scales Moor the obelisk resides, a classic example of how a boulder can be moved to a completely different location by the retreating ice. One other oddity on these vast boulders is how the boulder itself, when sitting on exposed limestone, is often perched miraculously on a smaller bit of rock, on occasions one foot above. It is thought the softer limestone may have eroded under the harder gritstone and eventually the erratic will topple over and slip further down the mountain.

Limestone Features

1 Limestone hardly erodes through normal water erosion but when it falls as rain the water picks up carbon dioxide, becomes acidic, reacts and with the abrasive efforts of moving glaciers or freeze/thawing, dissolves the rock over time to form fissures.

2 The most obvious initial signs of this erosion is the formation of limestone pavements. The fissures (or grikes as they are commonly known) form between blocks of rock to form the pavements. There is a wonderful example of a limestone pavement at Southerscale Scars near Chapel le Dale and on the descent of Ingleborough.

3 Limestone scars have formed across the steeper mountain sides where the rock has become exposed and scraped by water erosion. The rock crumbles and forms the distinctive rock falls under the scars. The speed of this erosion can sometimes be seen when the scar starts to collapse in to a dry stone wall above, it is a living and moving landscape.

4 The greatest consequence of the limestone bedrock is not what is above land but what is below. Where the fissures go deeper, the water and erosion starts to form underground rivers and passages, enlarging to caves and pot holes. Examples of pot holes include the famous Gaping Gill. Hull Pot however is an example of a sink hole where the land has not yet collapsed to form a pot hole but is still forming a spectacular waterfall. The Caving network is discussed in more detail on pages 80 to 83.

5 I am often asked "what is a shake hole?" mainly because it is one of the most referenced features on an Ordnance Survey map. Really it is a shallow crater formed where the mud and scale on top of the limestone has been washed away, down a fissure at the bottom of the crater.

The entrance to Gaping Gill

History, Geology and Land Usage

Man's Early Influence

Deforestation: Great forests covered the Dales and most of northern Britain 8,000 years ago. It was predominantly a mix of birch and pine, not as good for building material but excellent as a habitat for animals, insects, flora and a range of wildlife. Our mild and wet climate added to the mix making the soils perfect for a flourishing life.

Clearing the Land: However only about 4% of the land in the Dales is now under woodland (broadleaf or conifer). The decline has been the direct result of the actions of man, starting in the Stone Ages (Neolithic times). Bearing in mind most of the trees were cut by hand held axes it is an extraordinary achievement.

St Oswald's Church, Horton

Farmers clearing land for planting vegetables or grazing horses and other animals started the decline but increased during the Bronze and Iron Ages when the wood was used for timber builds, ship making and fuel.

Introduction of Sheep: Once the trees were gone the nutrient rich soils were altered, the water became waterlogged and the oxygen reduced. The soils became increasingly acidic and any kind of farming or tree growth very difficult without the addition of alkaline based fertilizers. With crop growing being an increasingly difficult activity the locals in medieval times started to turn to sheep farming as a predominant activity. The acid soils were problematic for sheep but the introduction of lime fertilizers helped establish sheep. Any re-introduction of trees has to be carefully managed with sheep kept well clear or they will eat the seeds.

Landscape Today: The deforestation of the Dales landscape has led to the landscape we see today. The moorlands which cover nearly 50% of the Dales do offer a rich habitat for many rare birds (such as hen harrier, merlin, golden plover and lapwing) and offer places for the introduction of rare animals such as red squirrels. Unfortunately, the lack of trees has reduced many natural habitats, created flood risk problems due to increased run off and created the familiar landscape of today.

Place Names and Word Origins

The origin of place names often gives a character to that place. It also tends to indicate the history and development of that place. Rivers and hills tend to have the oldest names as they had most relevance to people at the time. However nearly all the Dales names around the 3 Peaks area came from either an Anglo Saxon or Viking origin.

In general anything ending in 'ton' or 'ham' is Anglo Saxon whilst 'by' is Vikings. It is Vikings who introduced words for the most commonly used geographical features: dale (valley), force (waterfall), beck (stream), thwaite (a clearing) and gill (small mountain stream).

Ingleborough: "fortification on the peak hill". Old English 'burgh' being the fort and 'ingle' the peak hill as with Ingleton.

Whernside: "The hill where millstones (querts) are got". Anglo Saxon.

Pen-y-Ghent: Origin unknown except 'Penno' which is the Celtic word for hill. The popular name 'hill of the winds' is incorrect, referenced by a 19th century writer. It feels Celtic in origin and may mean 'hill of the border land'.

River Ribble: "The Boundary". Old English origin. The river forming the western boundary of Craven.

Ribblehead: "The source of the river/boundary".

Horton-in Ribblesdale "the farmstead on the dirty land". The 'ton' comes from 'tun' and is a popular Anglo Saxon reference for places in the 9th and 10th centuries.

Ingleton: "the farm near the peak hill". 'ton' referring to the original farm, Anglo Saxon origin.

Clapham: "the homestead on the noisy stream" Old English.

Chapel le Dale: "the chapel in the dale". The original chapel was Norman/French, thus 'chapelle'. Dales is Anglo Saxon, originally from Germany.

Norber: "north hill". A combination of Old English and Norse.

Hull Pot: "the pot hole near the hut". The pot is from medieval times but the hull/hut is an earlier origin? Was there a hut/farm nearby?

History, Geology and Land Usage

Sheep Farming

Sheep have been in our country since Roman times, reaching their hiatus in Medieval times when their wool, meat, skins and milk formed the basis of all trade. Today meat is the most important product but fleece and milk still have their own markets.

The wool was most valuable in the 13th century when it drove an economic boom in rural areas, prior to the invention of any synthetic fibres. Much of the farming land was owned by the abbeys of the area, Bolton Abbey estate being a large landowner but so too Fountains Abbey which managed 15,000 sheep. The land was divided up into pockets of land which local peasants ran on behalf of the landowner.

From the 17th century the peasants started to be awarded some rights and became tenants of the land owners, by this time the influence of the abbeys had waned and large landowners owned the land (in many cases a forerunner of today). These tenant farmers paid a rent to the landlord and started to enclose their land with stone walls more effectively. They also built some of the original stone barns to live in, often sleeping above their animals. In the mid 18th century the enclosure act formalised the building of field boundaries and led to the dry stone walls which so characterise the landscape of today.

A 'Dalesbred' on the descent from Whernside

Although wool production started to decline a century or so ago the meat from sheep (and their lambs) continued to be popular. It is only in the last 30 years that the returns have dropped, coincidently when the supermarkets started to drive down the prices that they paid farmers and produce from abroad became more widely available and cost effective.

Today sheep farming in the upland areas is in itself rarely sustainable to the farmers. Many now diversify or rely on subsidies and support from the outside to survive. However these upland farmers provide a valuable job in the preservation and development of our inspirational landscape. The upkeep of walls and stone barns, the use of sheep to stop the lands rewilding and the preservation of a traditional industry all help the growth of such industries as tourism, now the area's biggest employer.

Yorkshire 3 Peaks

Traditional Stone Barns

There are estimated to be over 4,000 stone barns in the Dales, along with the dry stone walls, creating the unique scenery of the area. Stone built barns replaced the original timber barns from the start of the 18th century. They tended to be situated away from the main farm buildings so that any transport of the hay and muck was limited, best to be on the spot.

- Many of these stone barns had a dual purpose, cattle below and winter hay storage above.

- Others were known as hogg barns and housed sheep during the winter months, often over 2 levels.

Today they are less used for their traditional purposes, often derelict and falling into disrepair. The National Park will give planning permission for development with strict rules both in maintaining the original style and stone work and usage. Local cottage businesses, local housing and short stay visitor accommodation must be combined with easy access to gain approval.

Along with the 5,000 miles of dry stone walls, the stone barns form a landscape that should be full of interest for any walker in the area. You cannot miss them!

A traditional Dales barn

History, Geology and Land Usage

Settle to Carlisle Railway

One of the memories any walker takes away after completing the 3 Peaks is the Settle to Carlisle Railway and in particular the Ribblehead Viaduct. The railway is 72 miles long with the most scenic section passing through the Yorkshire Dales between Settle and Kirkby Stephen. Heading north from Horton the line passes between Pen-y-Ghent and Ingleborough and then bending to a more north easterly direction to avoid running directly into Whernside.

The most iconic feature is the exceptional Ribblehead Viaduct lying bang in the middle of all 3 Peaks. In addition I must admit to a fascination with the tunnel at Blea Moor, an even more extraordinary feat of Victorian engineering.

Not only does the railway greatly enhance the 3 Peaks experience from an aesthetic viewpoint but it also has practical uses, especially when the party splits and certain members wish to cut short the walk!

Blea Moor station

Steam Trains

Recently I was with a 3 Peaks group at Blea Moor Tunnel and we watched a steam train as it disappeared in to the tunnel. It was a lovely experience and lifted the weary limbs for the pull up Whernside.

There are quite often steam trains on the Settle Carlisle Railway but they are operated by private companies and it is difficult to find any schedules so you can plan your visit. The Fellsman, Dalesman and the Flying Scotsman all travelled the line during 2018 so google them and you may find a time when they are running.

History of the Railway

In the mid 19th century the growth and popularity of railways was at its highest. A number of different rail companies were competing for business (sounds familiar!) and the Midland Railway Company in particular were looking for a slice of the lucrative Anglo Scotland market.

Although the main east and west coast lines existed the Midland Company were trying to operate a line to connect from Skipton towards the west coast line via Ingleton. However they could not get an agreement to share Ingleton Station and the LNWR were generally obstructive and difficult. The Midland Railway Company decided in 1865 the best option was to create a new line through the Dales to Carlisle.

Construction started in 1870 and was completed in 1876. What is important to realise is that the line was built for high speed passengers to compete with the main east and west coast lines, not for local travel. Therefore the route passed the easiest gradients, and resulted in 17 major viaducts the three quarter of a mile long tunnel at Blea Moor and stations that were built for speed, not local convenience.

Great for tourists now, less convenient for the local populations of Kirkby Stephen and in particular Dent where the station is 4 miles and 600ft higher than the village!

The 'Beeching' Act

Voted recently the second most scenic railway in the world (after the Blue Train in South Africa) the line was nearly closed for good in the 1970s as part of the Beeching Report. Many 'unprofitable' stations across Britain were closed as passenger numbers dropped and freight became a more important illustration of a line's profitability. Lack of investment did not help and notice was given in 1984.

However a local campaign led by the newly formed Friends of Settle Carlisle Railway persuaded the government to keep the line running. It was found that not only were passenger numbers underestimated (and some deliberately diverted away from the line) but that estimates given by British Rail were deliberately inflated including repairs to Ribblehead Viaduct. Coupled with a strong local campaign and an increase in passenger traffic, Michael Portillo announced in 1989 that the threat of closure had been lifted.

The second most scenic railway line in the world had been saved and thrives today.

History, Geology and Land Usage

100 ft high arches on the Ribblehead Viaduct

Ribblehead Viaduct

At one stage 6,000 railway workers (navvies) were working on the line, temporary camps/villages grew up and many people died as a result of the dangerous working conditions, disease and the rough conditions.

The largest of these villages was at Batty Green (the local name for Ribblehead at the time) which housed 2,000 workers. The viaduct is 400m long with 24 enormous arches (every 6th pillar is 50% thicker to support any collapse) up to 100ft tall. The construction took 4 years and involved small construction sites and mini rail lines transporting the limestone masonry making up the majority of the viaduct.

Over 100 people died on the construction of the viaduct which resulted in the Midland Company expanding the graveyard at nearby Chapel le Dale to cope. The Church of St Leonards is just one of a number of memorials to the dead. What is particularly thought provoking is the number of children who died in these camps where the conditions were atrocious.

The viaduct stands in memorial to Victorian engineering, the magnificent and the abominable.

Blea Moor Tunnel

From Ribblehead the walker on the 3 Peaks Challenge walks alongside the rail track for nearly 2 miles before crossing and heading up the steep slopes of Whernside. This is the point where the line disappears into Blea Moor Tunnel, the second extraordinary example of Victorian engineering. The tunnel is 1.5 miles long and at its deepest 500ft below the surface. Due to its length 7 construction tunnels were built from the lands above, this allowed 16 groups of construction workers to be in the tunnel at any one time. Three of these are still used today as ventilation shafts for the railway.

Rumour has it that the ghost of a long dead construction worker stalks the tunnel. Personally I can believe it, anyone who has walked past the signal box at the nearby Blea Moor station will understand. With dusk falling, or the mist and cloud down it is a spooky place, I would happily wild camp in most places in Britain but not near Blea Moor!

Protecting the Footpaths Today

Repairing the Bruntscar path on Whernside

Yorkshire 3 Peaks

New path high on Pen-y-Ghent

In 1986, a study by the Institute of Terrestrial Ecology (ITE) described the 3 Peaks area as having the sad distinction of possessing 'the most severely eroded footpath network in the UK'. In response, the Yorkshire Dales National Park Authority established its first Three Peaks Project. 33 years on, the project is still going strong – but it now has a very different focus.

Alan Hulme is head of Park Management and has shared his thoughts on pages 66 and 67.

Three Peaks Project

The Three Peaks project provides users of the route an opportunity to give something back to the area they love.

The money raised enables one Ranger to be specifically employed to maintain the routes.

There are many ways this is being done, event organisers make a 'donation' based on £1 per participant for events held in the area. The Authority also receives donations directly through its website from other events and organisations. Some businesses in the area recognise the revenue Three Peaks walkers generate for their business, and also give to the Three Peaks project.

There are also a wealth of different souvenirs and even an App that can be purchased from the Authority website with all the proceeds going back into the maintenance of the routes.

Protecting the Paths Today

The ITE's report three decades ago concluded that an estimated 41km of path was moderately to severely eroded. Developed in partnership with what was then English Nature, the Countryside Commission and the Sports Council, the initial Three Peaks Project was very much experimental.

Historical Context

Initially aggregate paths could be built successfully by floating them over the most severely damaged peat, subsoil paths (where conditions allowed) were a more cost-effective solution, and constructed paths and damage to the sides could be effectively revegetated through seeding and other vegetation restoration works, including just letting nature take its own course.

Major advances in tackling path erosion and habitat restoration were made, with a total of 14km of path being repaired and an area of 38,000m2 reseeded. However, at the end of the project in 1992, work estimated at a value of £469,000 (at April 1992 prices) was still required to address the remaining erosion issues in the area. As a result the Authority began a new era of Three Peaks Projects.

Between 1992 and 2004 three further externally-funded Three Peaks Projects were managed by the National Park Authority. In excess of £2 million was invested in the public rights of way network. Building on the experience gained in the original project, this investment largely focused on the installation of 'engineered routes' able to sustain the levels of user pressure, whilst being sensitive to their open upland environment.

The usual rule of thumb is to look to implement the lowest form of intervention but many of the routes were or are already severely damaged and as such more engineered solutions have had to be found (see opposite page).

The two photos below show what can be achieved. They show a flagged path to the east of Pen-y-Ghent, before and after.

The 4 Techniques used to repair a footpath

There are four specific ingredients that influence what can and can not be done today if the paths have reached a stage where the natural surface cannot be maintained. These are the underlying geology, hydrology, gradient and level of use that dictate what construction method are considered.

1. **Aggregate Paths**

These tend to suit the level sections of the route, on shallow or deep peat. Aggregate can be floated on a geotextile (a two or three dimensional material similar to a roll of cloth) or a geogrid (plastic grid lattice). The latter tend to be far superior on the deeper peat soils where levels of use are high for example at Hunt Pot, Pen-y-Ghent.

2. **Subsoil Paths**

This technique literally turns the route of the path upside down. It is therefore, absolutely dependent on the quality of the subsoil which is brought to the surface and shaped to create an even surface. This technique allows for the surface to naturally vegetate (or with help from seeding) and thus create a route with a more sustainable and natural appearance. Where levels of use have been high further drainage works and top dressing with an aggregate provide a harder wearing surface, such as on Simon's Fell Breast, Ingleborough and sections of the accents/decents of Whernside.

3. **Stone Pitched Paths**

This technique is most suitable to use on sloping sites with gradients in excess of 30 degrees. Stone pitching relies on the laying of mass stone. The stones are positioned vertically and dug into the soil so that approximately two thirds of the stone is below original ground level. This is a widely used method in the UK uplands and has recently been implemented at Bruntscar, Whernside.

4. **Stone Flagged Paths**

These have in some circumstances replaced the conventional boardwalks, but are still used when conditions are extremely wet. This can be seen on the lower section of Ingleborough where the traditional timber boardwalk remains. Above that the original oak flex boards have been replaced with stone flags. The area is National Nature Reserve and the flags rest on top of the peat vegetation which helps support them. It also means they could be removed if required. Stone flags have also been used in different ways, for example on Pen-y-Ghent near to the summit. On the west side looking down to Horton these have been placed to form a series of steps on what is a very steep gradient rather than laying level, as on the east side of the summit looking across to Fountains Fell.

History, Geology and Land Usage

Tradiitional Dales scenery

Yorkshire 3 Peaks

A Landscape for the Future

"If farmers and land owners left the Dales and the lands returned to undrained bog and upland scrub would tourists still come to the area or indeed would people want to live here?"

The simple answer to the question is 'in reduced numbers' but this disguises a deeply complex question. The landscape of the Yorkshire Dales, and in particular around the 3 Peaks, is unique in Britain. The rolling uplands of short grass, dry stone walls, barns, sheep and limestone outcrops are the iconic image that is conjured up when imagining the Dales. Wide valleys and pretty villages complete the picture. It is beloved of photographers and painters and most often used to promote the area.

Picturing yourself walking alongside a dry stone wall and finishing with a pint in a traditional Yorkshire pub brings thousands of people to the area, more so than any other image. The image does not age and in this time of increasing health consciousness it will only grow.

Rewilding

However, this picture perfect landscape is only 'natural' in terms of its geological shape, everything else is man-made. Remove the sheep from the fields, ban grouse shooting in the upper moors and stop repairing the walls/field barns and within 20 to 30 years the landscape would look very different. Nature will return, wild scrubland will start to encroach the tamer landscape we see and bogs will start to form in the valleys and the land will start to revert to how it was 2,000 years ago. Although this may not sound appealing this natural habitat will soon attract more and varied birdlife, wildlife and insects. If you are in any doubt go and visit the old quarry above Ribblehead station. Trees and forests will eventually claim the valley floor. There is a place for rewilding but let's not destroy our heritage.

Farming and tourism have to work together to provide the employment and benefit the economy of the area, they are not mutually exclusive to each other. It does not always feel that way today. Conflict occurs when badly informed visitors impact with distrustful landowners.

Lets preserve this special area, landowners, residents and visitors alike.

Not Just for Walkers

3 Peaks Challenge

Approaching Whernside

Not Just for Walkers: Biking

Cycling on Twisleton Scar

Yorkshire 3 Peaks

David Wild's passion is exploring the Dales, or any hills and mountains really, something he has done for many years. He enjoys all forms of cycling and often tells me what a great invention the bicycle is! It's perfect for exploring the Dales at any age. Whether on the winding country lanes that criss-cross the area or off-road on the many trails. He particularly likes going on long off-road journeys, and for that his preferred option is a 29er hardtail mountain bike, the lighter the better.

Cycle Cross on the 3 Peaks

38 miles/61km, 5,000 feet of climbing. The race takes between 3 and 5 hours and is run in September.

Recognised or at least marketed as the toughest Cyclo Cross event in the UK, this is for professionals and well versed amateurs. A cyclo-cross bike is a road bike with cyclo-cross tubulars/tyres and low gears and is the only type of bike acceptable in the race.

The route starts and finishes at Helton Bridge and reverses the traditional route (starting up Ingleborough and finishing on Pen-y-Ghent). It does not follow the walkers route for much of the time, which is a blessing, due to the nature of the ground, and visits Ingleton as an 'extra'.

18 miles are on the road and an additional 20 are off road. The final 5 off road miles are deemed 'uncyclable' with many carrying their bikes.

Not Just for Walkers: Biking

David Wild Says...

"It may seem old fashioned, but if you like perusing maps, a good way to start is with a highlighter pen and a map of the 3 Peaks area. Pick out all the by-ways and bridleways and you will see that there is quite an extensive network of tracks to ride on. It is possible to plan your own routes to circumnavigate each of the three peaks, Whernside, Ingleborough and Pen-y-Ghent. There are short linking sections of road required for each route but, on the whole, these are nice quiet lanes and so do not detract too much from the journey.

A mountain bike is probably the preferred option for riding in the area, but having said that, many of the tracks are suitable for a cyclo-cross or gravel bike. As riders will know, the distances that you can cover in a day are easily 3 to 4 times what you would manage if walking.

Cycle Cross 2019 (Ade Gidley)

Each of the 3 Peaks can be circumnavigated by routes ranging from around 15 to 35 miles. In all cases linking sections on busy roads can be avoided. Unfortunately, the only summit of the 3 Peaks that can be reached on a bridleway is Ingleborough. That would be an out and back journey from Ingleton on a medium to hard route. Probably better, riding across the eastern flank of Whernside on a good grass path with views across to Ingleborough is a must do section. Alternatively, the large track from near the centre of Horton in Ribblesdale takes you by Hull Pot, always an interesting place to stop. It may make you wonder what could be beneath your wheels as you cross the area!

Yorkshire 3 Peaks

Pennine Bridleway

The Pennine Bridleway runs through the centre of the area. To my mind it is a great route for getting miles under your wheels. Most of the riding is moderate on good surfaces. The track goes through some wonderful limestone scenery. Starting from Austwick or Clapham you are soon into the dramatic limestone pavement area above Crummack Dale, always worth stopping to take in the view. Through Sulber, which in spring can put on a show of quite rare wild flowers, and over the Ribble Valley. As you climb up out of the Ribble Valley heading east and north you eventually come across Ling Gill, a miniature National Nature Reserve and SSSI for its sub-alpine ash woodland. At the top of the gill there are a series of small weirs and a nice flat grassy area.

Further Afield

If you take the Pennine Bridleway up to Cam End it is then easy to link across into the tracks to the south of Hawes and Bainbridge. Some good tracks in this area take you around Semer Water. A note of caution though, some of the byways used by motorcycles and 4WD vehicles can become quite broken up, so be prepared for hard going in places.

A little further afield there are some great tracks around the Malham Tarn area. One of my favourites is the descent from The Weets down to Winterburn Reservoir.

Harvey's publish mountain biking maps of the area with the routes colour coded for the degree of difficulty, there are also a number of guide books that cover the area well."

Not Just for Walkers: Fell Running

Leaders approaching Whernside

Yorkshire 3 Peaks

Paul Baker is a keen walker and fell runner. In 2012 he decided to attempt the Yorkshire 3 Peaks fell race. This is a tough race for fit runners and demands some experience of fell running. The detailed entry qualifications are shown on the threepeaksrace.org website. The cut off times at High Birkwith, Ribblehead and the Hill Inn are about half the average times for walkers. In the end Paul ran the race twice, improving his time to 4 hours 23 mins at the second attempt. He tells his story on the next two pages.

2019 race at Ribblehead

Fell Race Statistics

The race record of 2 hours 46 mins was set by Andy Peace in 1996 and the women's record of 3 hours 9 mins by Victoria Wilkinson in 2017.

The Yorkshire Three Peaks race was first run in 1954. In that year there were six starters and only three finishers, now there are about 800 runners each year. The race is billed as the 'Marathon with Mountains' as it takes runners 23.3 miles over the summits of Pen-y-Ghent, Whernside and Ingleborough with 5,300ft of ascent and descent. The course is fundamentally the same as the walk but there are certain variations, the main one being the more direct ascent of Whernside from Ribblehead, which is used on race day only.

Not Just for Walkers: Fell Running

Paul Baker Says...

"Race records were not my concern as I struggled up the last few hundred metres of Whernside in 2012. It was more of a fell crawl than a Fell Race as I and other competitors were forced to pull ourselves up on hands and feet. The path levelled out at the top and after 'dibbing in' my electronic timer at the checkpoint I broke into a jog feeling confident I had the race beaten. Thirty seconds later I was lying on my back with cramp searing my calves.

I had wanted to have a go at running in, and hopefully completing, the Three Peaks Fell Race since my road running hobby had led me to try out cross country and local trail races. I had walked the Yorkshire 3 peaks a few times, initially as a teenager, but running it was a whole different prospect.

Start and finish of the 2019 race at Horton

The first challenge was to meet the qualifying criteria. For me this involved taking part in fell races of sufficient length and ascent. Being Birmingham based, the closest races were either Shropshire or the Black Mountains in Wales. What I learned from these qualifying races was; firstly, however you decide to carry the minimum kit required (waterproofs, compass, food, map etc), it always feels uncomfortable and, secondly, if you do most of your running on the road, the hills are going to be really painful.

The Route

The Yorkshire Three Peaks Fell Race follows the anti clockwise route, starting and finishing in Horton. It is held at the end of April, which means that it avoids bad winter weather but is prone to April showers. I discovered this 40 minutes after the 10am start as I approached the first peak, Pen-y-Ghent, and was reminded just how unpleasant a hail storm is when you are wearing shorts and struggling up a mountain.

Yorkshire 3 Peaks

Once past Pen-y-Ghent the weather improved and fortunately stayed like that for the rest of the day. Previously, when walking the route I had found navigation challenging on the long section from Pen-y-Ghent summit to Ribblehead but today, with plenty of runners to follow, it was not a problem. My main concern was the cut off 2 hours 10mins from the start at Ribblehead Viaduct. This is the second of three cut off points at the race, the third being at Hill Inn 3 hours 30 mins from the start.

I managed to pass the cut off with some time to spare but cramping up at the top of Whernside had me worried. Fortunately a fellow runner gave me some medical support (bending my feet back) and moral encouragement (get up and run or words to that effect!) and I was able to get going again. Descending Whernside was tricky but I managed to pass the last cut off within the scheduled time so now I was going to finish, whatever happened.

The climb up Ingleborough involved crossing the duckboards and then rock cut steps. It occurred to me that by this time the winner would have finished and be onto his second pint or protein recovery drink. Soon though I had ticked off the summit of Ingleborough and was on the deceptively long descent to Horton. It was made longer by further problems with cramp which eased a little after the first mile of descent.

After what seemed like hours descending from Ingleborough, I crossed the train line and entered Horton. I staggered up the finishing straight but my grimace was really a smile as, after all these years, I had completed the Three Peaks race in just under five hours, 4 hours 53 mins to be precise. The other plus was that the organisers had put on a brilliant beer tent."

Whernside in the background

Not Just for Walkers: Caving

Voldemort Pot (courtesy of Dales Guiding)

Yorkshire 3 Peaks

John Cordingley has kindly written a few words on the unique caving opportunities beneath the 3 Peaks and surrounding areas. He remains an active caver after more than four decades, with involvement in many discoveries in the Yorkshire Dales and elsewhere. He is currently working on a search for the large cave system which must lie behind Malham Cove. John served on the British Cave Rescue Council for 27 years and recently co-wrote an award winning book on Yorkshire Dales caving; https://www.wildplaces.co.uk/adventures-underground-book.

Gaping Gill

129 metres long, 31 metres high and 25 metres wide with water from Fell Back crashing 100 metres into the cavern.

Perhaps the most spectacular way of visiting the very heart of a famous cave system, with no special equipment or training, is at one of the two annual Gaping Gill public winch meets. These are run by the Bradford Pothole Club (late May) and the Craven Pothole Club (mid August). You'll descend almost 100m by bosun's chair into the huge Main Chamber, where cavers will explain the history of how the cave system was explored and tell you about where all the passages go.

Not Just for Walkers: Caving

John Cordingley Says...

"Surely the finest cave systems in the British Isles.

The first systematic cave explorations in the 3 Peaks area began almost two Centuries ago. All of the public section at Ingleborough Cave was found in 1837 (Queen Victoria's coronation year) and the earliest attempts to descend the great pothole of Gaping Gill came not long afterwards. Towards the end of the 19th Century the Yorkshire Ramblers Club was formed, with caving as a major part of its activities. However, what really kick started widespread underground work was the first complete descent of Gaping Gill in 1895 by a Frenchman, Edouard Martel. He showed that the "impossible" was really quite feasible and caving has been regularly pursued hereabouts in all the decades since.

Nowadays this western corner of the Yorkshire Dales is home to our nation's longest cave (the Three Counties Cave System near Ingleton, around 90km in length) but a great many other magnificent caves are known, as far to the east as Nidderdale and to the north, well beyond Swaledale.

The Beehive in Ingleborough Cave

The Jewel in the 3 Peaks Crown

The caving community has many real characters; often they come across as "rough diamonds" but beneath the facade these are the sort of people whom you can (and frequently do) trust with your life. They're often met in cafes and pubs in the area, loudly discussing the weekend's plans, or some hard won discovery.

My own caving began whilst at school; it opened up a different world, which I've never regretted devoting time to ever since. There are discomforts; sometimes hard physical effort and cold, cold water. But the rewards are beyond price; cavers witness exquisite calcite formations and beautiful rock architecture sculpted by the relentless action of water which, in some cases, have been visited by fewer people than have stood on the Moon. Like many long term cavers, I've specialised in certain aspects of our pastime, particularly diving in water-filled caves. Most folk associate this with perceptions of danger but, done properly, it can be safer than driving a car on the road. The real satisfaction in cave diving comes from being able to draw on years of training and experience to operate safely in what amounts to many people's worst nightmare. Most of the work is done whilst planning beforehand; get this right and a dive lasting several hours should go like clockwork.

So how can the uninitiated discover the unique attractions of the caving world for themselves? What you must not do is just go wandering into any caves you come across whilst walking, without skilled help. You may become the reason for a cave rescue, or unwittingly cause damage to the sensitive cave environment. Many people enjoy their first underground experience in safety and comfort on a tour of the excellent show caves for which the area is justly famous. Ingleborough Cave (at Clapham) and White Scar Cave (near Ingleton) are both a "must". These have mains electric lighting and good paths, as does Stump Cross Cavern (further afield, between Grassington and Wharfedale), another fine show cave.

Those who want to try something a bit more energetic might consider the British Caving Association's "Try Caving" days. Many clubs co-operate in running these, which allow real caving trips to be enjoyed for hardly any outlay (just, for example, the hire of a lamp and helmet). You can, of course, approach a caving club directly; most are happy to recruit and look after new members. It is also possible to hire an instructor, accredited by the British Caving Association, perhaps to visit the stream caves around Ribblehead or the famous Long Churn Caves near Selside. Contacts for caving clubs or instructors can be found online, or by asking in the various specialised caving equipment shops in the area.

What better inspiration could there be than this, to give caving a go yourself?"

Entrance to Ingleborough Cave

Beyond the 3 Peaks

The Yorkshire 3 Peaks

Pen-y-Ghent from Fountains' Fell

Beyond the 3 Peaks

So Much More to Enjoy in the Dales

One of the great frustrations I have living in the Dales is the emptiness of much of our outdoor lands. On many walks I have not seen a soul, even at weekends. Much as I personally like the feeling of remoteness and freedom I feel frustrated that there are not more people out there enjoying the wonderful walking the area has to offer. Actually I enjoy seeing a few people out and about; having a quick chat about the weather, the route etc livens up the day.

That is not to say I would like the area over run but there is a long way to go before we get to that stage. The Dales lives very much by the 95/5 rule where 95% of walkers are on the walks near Malham, Ingleton and Aysgarth. Alternatively a quick 5 minutes from my home village of Long Preston and there is nobody.

Summit of Great Knoutberry

This is even more extreme when it comes to the higher lands and moors further afield from the population centres. Aside from the 3 Peaks themselves it is rare to see anyone one. It does not happen in the Lake District where people are more spread out (even in the western valleys) but for a variety of reasons the majority of 'serious' walkers never get beyond the 3 Peaks. Don't get me wrong, the 3 Peaks are a fantastic day out and undoubtedly 'offer the finest one day challenge in England' but there are a number of other superb walks in the area that are explored in the next few pages.

The Yorkshire 3 Peaks

New Walking Challenges

Most people complete the 3 Peaks challenge and never return.

However the following pages detail just a small selection of the excellent challenges available for those who enjoy the area and are looking to return.

Wharfedale 3 Peaks: A much quieter '3 Peaks' option is in Upper Wharfedale, completing 3 mountains over 2,000ft high.

The Dales 30 Mountains: Most of the mountains in the Dales (Yorkshire and Cumbrian) are rarely visited, a new challenge that can be completed in a single week long walk or over time.

Other Challenging Walks: The Dales moors are vast empty playgrounds for the walker, enjoy them and gain a better feel for the area.

Long Distance Trails: Some of the finest long distance walks (trails) criss cross the country, offering the opportunity to head out in to a different landscape every day.

How Can We All Help?

It's almost as though the area is hiding its greatest charms. Having completed the 3 Peaks Challenge the first thing that should be encountered is a noticeable information board in the car park at Horton detailing the different challenges in the area. Here is a captive audience of people (up to 100,000 in 2018) who are about to or have completed the major challenge in the area and are almost certainly enthused about the thought of doing another.

Add more prominance to walking challenges other than the 3 Peaks on local information websites and other literature.

Certainly the various authorities and other private companies promotion of the Yorkshire Dales as a walking destination could be improved. If they all put as much enthusiasm in to walkers as cyclists just watch the numbers rocket!

Wharfedale 3 Peaks

A 2nd "Yorkshire 3 Peaks" Challenge

Great Whernside 704m (2,310ft)
Buckden Pike 702m (2,303ft)
Birks 610m (2,001ft)

The most obvious alternative to the Yorkshire 3 Peaks is the Wharfedale 3 Peaks. Over the years I have guided a number of parties around the head of Wharfedale and the walk is full of interest. The walk is shorter than the 3 Peaks but just as tough, the underfoot terrain is much rougher and navigation in bad weather is challenging.

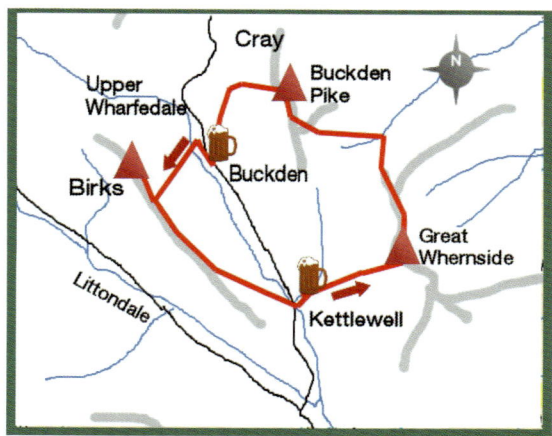

Kettlewell

This attractive grey stone village dominates Upper Wharfedale and is the perfect place to complete the Wharfedale 3 Peaks. The village originated as a base for farming but was soon dominated by the lead mines that are on the slopes of Great Whernside. Even today it is an active village, retains a village primary school and a very popular Scarecrow Festival held in mid August.

Kettlewell is an excellent base for the challenge, there is plenty of parking, a choice of 3 pubs and 2 further cafes, a campsite and a good shop selling more than just essentials. It is well set up.

Stage 1
Great Whernside

Climbing Great Whernside

1 From the main car park in Kettlewell, cross the bridge and turn immediately right before the Blue Bell Inn. Head up the road, past Zarinas, cross the road at the shop and continue with the river on your right. Where the road bears sharp left follow the footpath for 100m through houses at the east end of the village and cross a footbridge on your right.

2 Turn immediately left with the river on your left for 150m to a small stream. Cross the stream and looking uphill take the left forked footpath heading up the hillside. Climb steadily along a farm track passing through 2 gates before the path levels out. Great Whernside is directly ahead. The footpath (not now a track) passes through 4 dry stone walls before arriving at the building of Hag Dyke, a popular scout hostel with a chapel. Have a rest and look around.

The Yorkshire 3 Peaks

3 Leaving the hut on your left, cross a stile on to open hillside. Ahead is a steep climb to the summit of Great Whernside, a distance of 1km and nearly 250m. The summit of Great Whernside is a mass of millstone grit boulders which need to be picked through to arrive at the trig point and cairn. At the summit the views to the north and east open out in a large arc of remote moorland, the crossing in to Nidderdale being one of the roughest in Northern England.

4 Leave the trig heading north on the summit ridge keeping to the edge of the drop to the left. After 300m along the ridge turn just west of north. Follow for 1km to a wall and then take the descent to your left until meeting a stile over the wall. Cross the stile and carefully pick your way down some steep ground, heading north west.

5 The path turns gradually more west and becomes less steep. However this part of the walk is very wet and muddy so it is a question of picking your way to the road and keeping your feet as dry as possible.

Hag Dyke Scout hut in the distance

Wharfedale 3 Peaks

Stage 2
Buckden Pike

1 Cross the road (Kettlewell to Coverdale) and turn right for a few metres until a faint path heads up the hillside for 1.5km just north of west. The second half of this steady climb is alongside a wall. On meeting a 2nd wall follow the path just west of north as it climbs up the shoulder of Buckden Pike.

2 The ground here undulates, gaining height slowly, but keep the wall to your left and your feet dry. Follow the ridge for nearly 2km until it meets a 2nd path coming from the left near a junction of walls. Ignore the bridlepath heading due north and stick to the fainter path heading west up steeper slopes alongside a wall.

Polish War Memorial

3 As the climb finishes there is a large cross bedded in a concrete base. This is a Polish War Memorial erected in honour of a Polish training aircraft that crashed in WW2 killing all but one of its crew. The base retains fragments of the aircraft itself. At the cross, climb the stile over to the west side of the ridge and walk north for 1km to the summit of Buckden Pike.

Approaching Buckden Pike

4 The summit of Buckden Pike has a trig point and a large cairn with good views to the west over the Yorkshire 3 Peaks. To descend, head north for a few metres, and then take the left fork in the path that descends steeply on the south side of the wall. The path leaves the wall after the steepest section but is obvious as it turns to the left.

5 Heading initially west past some shake holes (craters in the ground) the path starts to bend in a more south west direction and contours the hillside. The hillside is littered with loose rock. Pass through four walls, either via a small gate or because the wall has collapsed, but at the fifth where the path meets a second path turn left and drop through a wooded area into the large car park at Buckden village. There are toilets and a small shop/café next to the car park.

Stage 3
Birks

Trig point (but not the high point) of Birks

1 From the car park at Buckden cross the main road and take the side road heading down to the river. Cross the road bridge and continue walking along the road for 500m. A footpath sign points up the farm track and almost immediately zig zags up the hillside. Pass some trees and a gate the track enters open ground. Walk south for a further 200m and at a stream turn right on to a faint path heading up the uniformly steady climb up Birks.

2 From the start of this footpath (actually a bridlepath) to the summit ridge is nearly 2km in length, 250m in height and in a steady direction just west of south. The path is usually clear to follow but in places it gets swallowed up in the wet ground. Just before the ridge is met some stone slabs have been laid to improve the walking.

3 On arrival at the summit wall the trig point to the left is the obvious point to aim for but sadly the real high point is 1.5km to the north along the ridge. The difference in height between the trig and high point is only 3m but that is enough. Stick to the wall, past an old shooting hut and Birks Tarn to your right to a small stile that leads over the wall to a pile of stones marking the high point of Birks.

4 From the summit return to the trig point of Birks and enjoy the lovely views of both the U shaped valleys of Wharfedale and Littondale. It is downhill all the way from here.

5 The return to Kettlewell is straightforward and pleasant. Keep to the ridge for 3km, following the line of a solid dry stone wall. Even where it kinks to the left after 1km follow it round and then go over a stile to continue along the ridge. After 3km the ridge is crossed by the second of 2 footpaths heading east. This one drops directly towards Kettlewell, passing through a limestone scar before meeting a farm track near the road bridge over the River Wharfe. Cross the bridge to the car park.

Near Birks summit

The Dales 30

Eyeing up Yarlside

The Yorkshire 3 Peaks

The Dales 30 are mountains over 2,000ft (610m) with a 30m (98.4ft) drop on all sides, defined in official mountain terminology as Hewitts.

Slopes of Calf Top, Barbondale

I liked the criteria because the 2,000ft height is the generally recognized division between hill and mountain whilst a minimum 100ft drop equated to 30 mountains and a suitable challenge. The geographic area is defined by the new boundary of the Yorkshire Dales National Park (as of 2016). However, many of the mountains are in Cumbria or Lancashire so I have referred to the area as 'The Dales'.

My reasons for enjoying the challenge are explained in the next four pages, including my three favourite 'Dales 30' mountains and a challenging 9 day walk that takes in all 30 in one continuous journey.

Buy the Book

The Dales 30 book is available via Where2walk for £12.95.

Start the challenge.

93

The Dales 30

Why Tackle the 'Dales 30'

The Dales 30 provides a completely different sort of challenge. A more leisurely challenge, one that can be done at one's own pace, involve multiple visits, can be done at any time of the year (and should be) and one that covers most of the area. It brings with it a full appreciation of the Dales. The 30 mountains all display different characteristics, have different approaches and involve different challenges.

Travelling at different times of the year certainly adds to the enjoyment of the challenge. Buckden Pike in the snow is a very different proposition to a leisurely amble on a long summer's day. It brings a sense of adventure and excitement that still gives me a thrill and at times a real burst of adrenalin. Between the two lie the wonderful colours of autumn and the pretty flowers, lambs and freshness that a bright spring day can bring.

The Dales 30 will take you to most of the corners of the Dales and to places you may not otherwise visit. The villages and buildings of the area are one of its greatest attractions. The Dales 30 will bring you to the lesser spotted Dent, the book town of Sedbergh, exquisite Upper Swaledale, underrated Kirkby Stephen as well as the more popular villages in Upper Wharfedale, Ribblesdale and the queen of market towns, Hawes. Planning a weekend away in Muker for example, climbing a couple of mountains and enjoying the evening in a traditional Dales pub surely ranks right up there with top weekend breaks in the world.

For me, a day on Yarlside was typical. A late summer's day, warm hazy weather, a hill I had not climbed before and a route I was not too sure of. Just what I like. For 30 minutes I enjoyed a leisurely stroll along the valley with the waterfall at Cautley Spout offering a spectacular backdrop. A steep climb had me sweating on Yarlside before a gentle wind cooled me as the slope flattened. For the next 45 minutes the going was perfect, easy going on short, soft grass as I followed the undulating ridge to Randygill Top. From here I sat and worked out an unusual route down, enjoying virgin territory near Wandale Fell. I picked my way through sheep, farms and a quiet beck before emerging again at Cross Keys Inn. I was happy to finish the walk with a pot of tea in this fascinating inn. Perfect.

Scotland has the Munros, the Lake District has the Wainwrights, let's hope the Dales 30 become as well known.

The Yorkshire 3 Peaks

1 Buckden Pike

At the head of Wharfedale lies Buckden Pike, steep sided and isolated from the mountains around. The summit area is a mile long ridge bookmarked with trig point and cairn at one one end and a memorial at the other end to the Polish airmen killed on a training flight in 1944. The pretty villages of Starbottor and Buckden complete a lovely day out.

Summit of Buckden Pike

2 The Calf, Howgills

The Howgill Fells lie between the Dales and the Lakes and are generally neglected in favour of their more famous neighbours. The mountains are in fact one large massif stretching for over 10 mles north to south with supero ridge walking along its spine and many satellite ridges. The Calf stands proud in the middle of the massif at its highest point.

Easy walking along the spine of the Howgills

3 Great Knoutberry

Great Knoutberry Fell lies at the head of Dentdale, commanding superb views down this rarely visited dale. The lower slopes of the mountain are dominated by the most picturesque section of the Settle Carlisle railway including Arten Gill viaduct and the highest station in England. The summit area is a perfect spot, short grass, great views and a stubby little trig point.

Arten Gill on the approach

The Dales 30 Challenge

Continuous Walk

201km (125 miles)

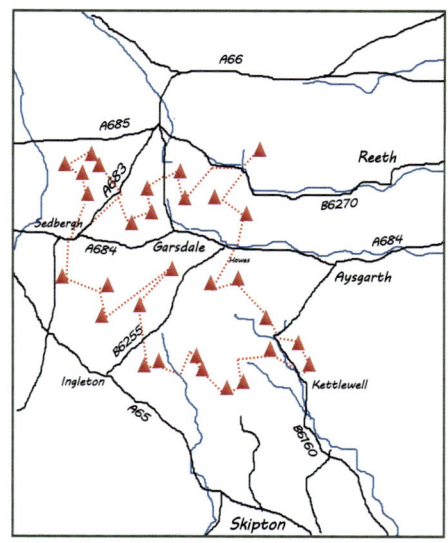

Completing the round of the Dales 30, 125 miles with 26,600ft of climbing, in a continuous walk of between seven and nine days, would be a fantastic challenge. There are paths over many of the sections, for example, Ingleborough, Penyghent, Whernside, Buckden Pike and The Calf, but there are parts of the walk, for example the seven mile west to east crossing of Yockenthwaite Moor, which are largely pathless. However, the terrain is not as rugged as parts of Scotland or the Lake District so reasonable progress can be made, even over the pathless sections.

Additionally there are places where the easiest and quickest route is not obvious, for example the ascent of Baugh Fell from Cautley, so route finding skills are required.

I suggest starting the round in either Sedbergh, Hawes, or Kettlewell. All three have excellent accommodation and pubs. In addition there is accommodation (pubs, guest houses and campsites) along the route, particularly at Keld, Horton in Ribblesdale and Dent.

A Proposed 9 Day Walk

Day 1. 12 miles, 3,500ft of climbing

Start at the car park in the centre of Sedbergh then climb Calders, The Calf, Fell Head, Randygill Top, Yarlside. Finish Cautley. Arrange a lift back to Sedbergh for the night or possibly stay at the Cross Keys.

Day 2. 12 miles, 3,000ft of climbing

Start Cautley, then Knoutberry Haw (Baugh Fell), Swarth Fell, Wild Baugh Fell. Transport would be required from the B6259 near Aisgill Farm to accommodation possibly at Hawes or Kirkby Stephen.

Day 3. 12 miles, 1,500ft of climbing

Start Aisgill Farm on B6259, then Little Fell, High Seat. Accommodation Keld.

The Yorkshire 3 Peaks

Day 4. 15 miles, 2,800ft of climbing
Start Keld, then Rogan's Seat, Great Shunner Fell, Lovely Seat. Accommodation Hawes.

Day 5. 14 miles, 2,300ft of climbing
Start Hawes, then Drumaldrace, Dodd Fell, Yockenthaite Moor. Accommodation possibly Buckden. Two additional miles if walking from the route to Buckden.

Day 6. 9 miles, 2,000ft of climbing
Start Buckden or near Cray Inn, then Buckden Pike, Great Whernside. Accommodation Kettlewell.

Day 7. 18 miles, 4,000ft of climbing
Start Kettlewell, then Birks Fell, Darnbrook Fell, Fountains Fell, Pen-y-Ghent, Plover Hill. Accommodation Horton in Ribblesdale.

Day 8. 19 miles, 5,000ft of climbing
Start Horton in Ribblesdale, Simon Fell, Ingleborough, Whernside, Great Knoutberry. Accommodation Dent.

Day 9. 14 miles, 2,500ft of climbing
Start Dent, Gragareth, Great Coum, Calf Top. Accommodation Sedbergh.

It is possible to combine Days 2/3 and Days 5/6 to make a 7 day challenge.

Summit of Whernside

Fell Running the Dales 30

It may be possible for a world class fell runner to complete the round in 24 hours, which would be an incredible achievement beyond my comprehension.
Similar to the Bob Graham Round in the Lake District the Dales 30 could become one of the great fell running challenges.

Other Challenging Walks

Moving Away From the Mountains

One of the many pleasures of walking in the Dales is the feeling that you have escaped the outside world. On the higher mountains (certainly the 3 Peaks) there are usually people, often in big groups. Move elsewhere in the Dales and, more particularly the large areas of high moorland, and that is very unusual. You can walk for hours and not see a soul, in fact it is quite exciting when you do!
The walks are not just remote they are full of interest. They offer a taste of the past. The dominant sheep farming of today, set in a landscape of stone walls, barns and pretty hamlets, is interspersed with remnants of old industries, forestry and of course tourism.

Overlooking Upper Nidderdale

The Yorkshire 3 Peaks

1 History in Swaledale

21km (13 miles)

Each main dale enjoys its own unique characteristic. Swaledale is many people's favourite. It may have a bleak feel to it due to the scarred fellside but this hides a fascinating history. The remnants of the lead mining industry, and some wild and exciting moorland walking make for a lovely day.

Near Surrender Bridge, Reeth

2 Explore Wensleydale

22.5km (14 miles)

There is much to see and do in the central dale of the area. A walk through Wensleydale is a walk with plenty to see, loads of variety and combines some moorland walking with a long riverside section. Aysgarth Falls, Bolton Castle, Carperby and Askrigg provide some of the best known highlights.

Typical walking near Aysgarth Falls

3 Heart of the 3 Peaks

24 kms (15 miles)

Rather than climbing the 3 Peaks walk through the remote countryside under their summits. The countryside is a mix of rough fields full of sheep, moorland and forestry mixed with hamlets and farms. The views towards the 3 Peaks themselves are interesting as they are viewed from unusual angles and heights.

On the Cam Road

Other Challenging Walks

The Yorkshire 3 Peaks

Walking through the village of Horton-in-Ribblesdale

Long Distance Walks

The Enjoyment of a Multi-Day Challenge

Long distance walks are becoming increasingly popular for walkers looking for new, tougher challenges. Being asked to walk day after day to a new destination is tough but many of us find it is very rewarding.

It is tough because it is relentless, each day has to be achieved whatever your physical condition and whatever the weather. Each day and area you are walking through is new and a navigational challenge (some routes are well signposted but many aren't, getting lost is almost inevitable albeit usually temporarily) and finding new accommodation each night is often difficult.

However the satisfaction is immense, a real challenge overcome. Each day is different, there are surprises around each corner and a shared comradeship when meeting others doing the same long distance walk. More than anything a long distance walk provides a much greater understanding of an area than a single base ever can.

The Yorkshire Dales has a number of long distance walks crossing the area. Most of these are linear and take in a chunk of the area. For example the Coast to Coast passes through Swaledale, the Dales Way passes through Wharfedale and Dentdale and the Pennine Way/Bridleway pass through its heart.

However, none of them focus solely on the Dales and get into the guts of the area except the Bracken Way. A new long distance route the 7 day Bracken Way focuses on the best bits of the Yorkshire Dales, beginning and ending at Settle. There is no waymarking (although it does stick to public footpaths) and the days are longer than the average long distance walk but it is without doubt the best way to discover and understand the area.

The route details for the Bracken Way are on pages 104/105.

The Yorkshire 3 Peaks

Dales Way

This is the best section of the Dales Way, the section from Sedbergh to Windermere is less good.

Ilkley to Burnsall - 13 miles

Burnsall to Kettlewell - 11 miles

Kettlewell to Ribblehead - 14 miles

Ribblehead to Dent - 13 miles

Dent to Sedbergh - 6 miles

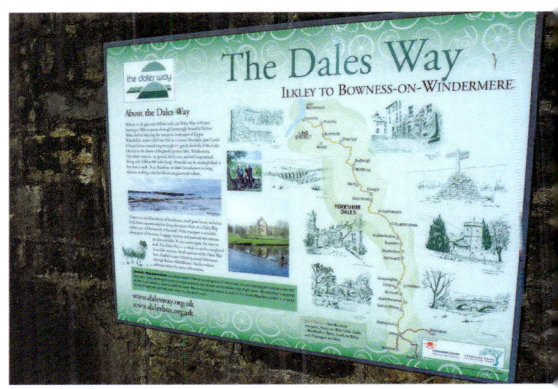

Pennine Way

.As part of an epic long distance trail (290 miles in total) the section through the Dales has some excellent sections and is tamer than some of the sections on either side.

Lothersdale to Malham - 15 miles

Malham to Horton - 14 miles

Horton to Hawes - 14 miles

Hawes to Keld - 12 miles

Keld to Bowes - 17 miles

Coast to Coast

The Coast to Coast passes through 3 National Parks of contrasting terrain with the Dales section starting in Mallerstang and heading down the complete length of Swaledale.

Shap to Kirkby Stephen - 18 miles

Kirkby Stephen to Keld - 12 miles

Keld/Thwaite to Reeth - 13 miles

Reeth to Richmond - 11 miles

Long Distance Walks

The Bracken Way

95 miles/7 Days

A multi-day walk visiting many of the best sites and countryside the Dales can offer.

To fully enjoy the Yorkshire Dales and, in particular to appreciate the variety and character of the individual dales, takes time. However in a week this can be comfortably achieved on foot.

I have put together a long distance route that visits the most interesting places in the Dales. The long distance footpath is called the Bracken Way after our old Border Collie (who would have loved it).

Try it and you will finish with a much better understanding and love for the 'Dales'

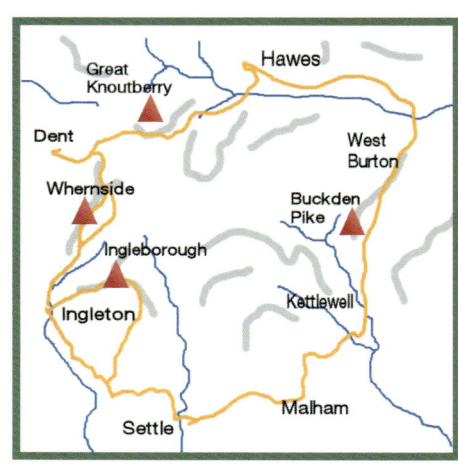

Racehorses Hotel, Kettlewell

Malham Cove

The Yorkshire 3 Peaks

Itinerary

Day 1. Settle to Malham

6 miles. A short first day with a pleasant walk over the limestone scenery of the Settle Loop to Malham. There is plenty of time for the 0.5 mile stroll to Malham Cove, often at its best in later evening light and a pint in one of the two delightful pubs.

Day 2. Malham to Kettlewell

13 miles. Head east to visit the waterfall Janet's Foss and the spectacular gorge of Gordale Scar. Head north to Malham Tarn before crossing some higher land to the lovely dale of Littondale. A final pull over a limestone shoulder and Kettlewell nestles below.

Day 3. Kettlewell to West Burton

14 miles. Buckden Pike is, in my view, the best mountain in the Dales. The route passes a few hundred feet from its summit. From Buckden Pike the route descends sharply into the lovely but rarely visited Walden Dale. The pretty village of West Burton awaits the tired walker at the end of the day.

Day 4. West Burton to Hawes

15 miles. The length of this day purely depends on how many places you want to visit. It is possible to include Castle Bolton, Aysgarth Falls, Askrigg and Hardraw Force before finishing the day in the market town of Hawes.

Day 5. Hawes to Dent

16.5 miles. The day includes some remote country as it leaves Yorkshire and continues in Cumbria. The path passes the lower slopes of Great Knoutberry and the fantastic viaduct at

Aysgarth Falls

Arten Gill on the Settle Carlisle railway. Cobbled streets greet the weary walker on arrival in the attractive village of Dent and the local micro brewery is very welcome.

Day 6. Dent to Ingleton

14.5 miles. From Dent the Bracken Way climbs out of Dentdale onto the slopes of Whernside. There is an option to climb the highest mountain in Yorkshire (maybe weather dependent) or skirt the mountain via Ribblehead Viaduct. The two routes meet above Ingleton waterfalls and then drop down to the town of the same name.

Day 7. Ingleton to Settle

14.5 miles. The final day is full of interest and variety. There is an option to climb Ingleborough, an excellent mountain or follow the lower route. The second part of the day passes the lovely villages of Clapham, Austwick and Feizor before arriving at Settle, the end of the walk.

Extra Information

Yorkshire Three Peaks Code of Conduct

The Yorkshire Three Peaks is part of the Yorkshire Dales National Park – a very special place.

The Three Peaks has become an increasingly popular location for fundraising events. **YOU** can help us keep the area special for everyone to enjoy by following the Yorkshire Three Peaks Code of Conduct:

Parking is Limited
- Keep vehicles to a minimum, use local transport to get here or car share where possible.
- Please park considerately and do not obstruct passing places, clearways, private roads, tracks, roadside verges, gateways or pavements.

Be Quiet!
- **Please keep noise to a minimum.** Respect the peace of people living and staying in the area.
- Keep early morning noise (from both people and vehicles) to an absolute minimum and maintain it until you are away from the village.
- Do not use bells or claxons to 'ring home' your participants at the end of their challenge.

Leave No Trace
Litter...
- **Take it home!** Litter places a burden on our small, rural communities and is a blight on the landscape. If you really want to help, pick up any odd bits you see along the way.
- **Remember,** banana skins and orange peel are litter, too – they are unsightly and take years to decompose.

Toilets...
- **Don't get caught short!** Toilet facilities on the Three Peaks route are limited (the only public toilets are at Horton-in-Ribblesdale).
- **Do not** use the mountains as an outdoor toilet. This has significant impact on local water supplies and ecology, and is unpleasant for other visitors. If you do need to urinate, do so at least 30m from streams and burns. If you need to defecate, do so as far away as possible from buildings, streams and farm animals. Bury faeces in a shallow hole and replace the turf.

Stay Safe
- **Be prepared!** Make sure you are well prepared in terms of kit and have a good level of fitness. Make sure you have at least one person in your group who can navigate in difficult conditions. Local mountain rescue teams are all volunteers and should only be called in an emergency.

Give Something Back
- **Support the local community** by using local facilities and services.
- **Donate to path maintenance.** Help us look after this special place by donating a minimum of £1 per walker - visit www.yorkshiredales.org.uk/threepeaks

Enjoy yourself – but please respect those who live and work here. Come back and stay some time soon, linger, explore and enjoy the local hospitality, and get to know the place and the people.

Let's keep the Yorkshire Three Peaks special

Horton-in-Ribblesdale Parish Council

YORKSHIRE DALES National Park Authority

Summit Ridge, Whernside

Accommodation

Broad Croft House
Horton in Ribblesdale

- Ideal location for people doing either the 3 Peaks or Pennine Way
- 5 luxury rooms, en-suite with lots of little extra's
- Extensive gardens as well free on site parking and WIFI

Room Types: 3 double/twin rooms in the house and 2 luxury pods in the garden.

Contact: 01729 860419 / 07715678918 or email marco.frik@yahoo.com

Visit: http://broadcrofthouse.co.uk/

Stackstead Farm
Ingleton

- Comfortable group accommodation for up to 22 people.
- 20 min drive to Horton in Ribblesdale, 10 minutes to Chapel le Dale.
- 5 minute walk to nearest pub

Room Types: Bunk Rooms for up to 22.

Contact: 01524241386 or email enquiries@stacksteadfarm.co.uk

Visit: http://www.stacksteadfarm.co.uk

Riverside Lodge GH

Ingleton

- Riverside location
- Sauna & Games Room
- Private car park

Room Types: 8 ensuite rooms inc doubles, twin and king size.

Contact: riversideingleton@gmail.com
01524 241359
Visit: http://www.stayatriverisde.co.uk

Boars Head

Long Preston

- Traditional pub close to the 3 Peaks
- Rooms from £80 (m/w) and £95 (w/e)
- Good food and excellent breakfast

Room Types: 6 rooms available. Twin/double, family and single rooms

Contact: 01729 840217 or
email boarsheadhotel@hotmail.co.uk

Visit: http://boarsheadlongprestor.co.uk/

Accommodation

Ferncliffe Guest House
Ingleton

- Village location where you will find a range of places to dine and shop.
- Ideally situated for walking, climbing, mountain biking and caving all from the doorstep.
- 4 miles from a 3 Peaks start

Room Types: Three Double Rooms and one twin/superking room.

Contact: 015242 41589
or email stay@ferncliffeguesthouse.co.uk

Visit: http://www.ferncliffeguesthouse.co.uk

Peaks and Pods
Rathmell, nr Settle

- High quality camping pods with WiFi, comfortable beds and stunning views of the beautiful countryside.
- Shared social space with wood-fired pizza oven, seating, lighting and fire pit
- A short drive to Horton to the start of the Three Peaks.

Room Types: Well equipped cedar clad pods, ensuite. Some with own hot tubs.

Contact: 07724 940709 or
email hello@peaksandpods.co.uk

Visit: https://peaksandpods.co.uk/

The Traddock Hotel
Austwick

- 14 luxury rooms and suites, a l en-suite with lots of little extra's.
- Bar, 2 dining rooms, 3 lounges. Set in extensive gardens with Wifi & parking
- A 10 minute drive from the start of the 3 peaks. Set under Ingleborough.

Room Types: 6 rooms available. Twin/double, family and single rooms

Contact: 015242 51224 or 07976 363833
email info@thetraddock.co.uk

Visit: https://www.thetraddock.co.uk/

The Dalesbridge
Austwick

- Extensive choice of accommodation.
- 15 min drive to Horton in Ribblesdale and Chapel le Dale.
- Cosy on-site bar (open at weekends) with log burner.

Room Types: 8 B&B, 8 Bunk Bed Cabins, 4 Glamping Pods and 100 camp pitches.

Contact: 015242 51021 or
email info@dalesbridge.co.uk

Visit: http://www.dalesbridge.co.uk

About the Author

Jonathan has lived and walked in the Dales for over 20 years. He is a qualified Mountain Leader with many years guiding under his belt including repeated circuits on the Yorkshire 3 Peaks. In 2000 he turned his passion into a career and set up Where2walk with the aim to make it the 'come to' website for anyone wanting to walk in the uplands of Britain.

The Where2walk website now describes over 500 individual walks, several long distance trails and a number of walking challenges including the Dales 30. Jonathan runs navigation courses in the Dales, offers a guiding service and sells walking holidays for those wanting to taste the pleasures of walking in our upland areas.

He self published his first book 'The Dales 30' in 2017 which has gained popular acclaim for introducing experienced walkers to different areas of the Dales.
Jonathan has completed the Munros (and Tops), the Wainwrights (twice) and will take any detour to find the highest point in the area.
It is rare to see him without his loyal border collie, Mist.